THE URBAN FAMILY

THE URBAN FAMILY

A Study of Hindu Social System

A.K. LAL

CONCEPT PUBLISHING COMPANY, NEW DELHI - 110059

ISBN 81-7022-295-8

First Published 1990

Awadhesh Kumar **Lal** (*b.* 1943)

Published by
Ashok Kumar Mittal
Concept Publishing Company
A/15-16, Commercial Block, Mohan Garden
NEW DELHI - 110059 (India)

Lasertypeset by
Microtech Advance Printing Systems (Pvt.) Ltd.
H-13, Bali Nagar, NEW DELHI - 110015

Printed in India by
Taj Press
Delhi-110006

Dedicated

to

Sri Dandi Baba

(Nanora Math, Belsand)

Contents

List of Tables 8

Preface 11

1. Introduction 13
2. Size and Composition of the Family 29
3. Division of Labour in the Family 38
4. Inter-Personal Relationship in the Family 48
5. The Structure of Power and Authority in the Family 61
6. Work and the Family 70
7. Changing Patterns of Marriage 79
8. Family and Class 101
9. Education and the Family 114
10. Summary and Conclusions 124

Bibliography 141

Index 149

List of Tables

1.1	Distribution of 1,000 Hindus according to Caste	22
2.1	Distribution of Families into Different Compositional Categories	32
2.2	Family Types among Upper and Lower Castes	33
2.3	Family Types and Educational Attainments of the Head of Households	34
2.4	Family Types and Monthly Income of the Families	35
2.5	Family Types and Age of the Heads of the Families	36
2.6	Size of the Family and Family Types	37
3.1	Family Types and Performance of Economic Duties by Males and Females together	40
3.2	Responsibility of Child Care and its Performance by various Types of the Families	41
3.3 (a)	Economic Activities of the Joint Family	43
3.3 (b)	Economic Activities in the Joint Family	44
3.4 (a)	Carrying the Responsibility of Child-Care in the Joint Family	45
3.4 (b)	Carrying on the Responsibility of Child Care in the Joint Family	46
4.1	Family Type of Percentage of Couples going out together to different Places	50
4.2	Extent of Avoidance between the Father-in-law and Daughter-in-law Relationship by Family Type	55
4.3	Family Type and the Pattern of Sibling Relationship	56
4.4	Mutual aid-pattern between Geographically separated Nuclear families of Parent and Children	59
5.1 (a)	Family Type and Perception of Final Authority by Respondents	64
5.1 (b)	Family Type and Perception of Final Authority by Respondents	65
5.2	Pattern of Decision-making by Family Type	69
6.1	Attitude of the Families of Different Types towards Educated Unemployed Males	71

6.2 Family Type and Preference for Education over Employment 74
6.3 Family Types and Attitude towards Manual Labour or the Job of Peon 75
7.1 Mean Age of Marriage for Males and Females Married during Different Period of Time 81
7.2 Mean Difference in the Age of Husband and Wife Married during Different Periods of Time 82
7.3 Mean Age of Marriage preferred for Boys and Girls 83
7.4 Mean of the Ages preferred for Marriage of Boys and Girls and the Family Type 84
7.5 Reaction of Parents towards Inter-Caste Marriage by Family Types 86
7.6 Family Type and Permissiveness to Love Marriage 89
7.7 Degree of Participation allowed to Men in Selection of their Mates 92
7.8 Family Type and Degree of Participation allowed to Males in Selection of Mates 92
7.9 Practice of Matching Horoscopes by Different Types of Families 93
7.10 Preference of Respondents of Different Family Types with regard to certain Specified Attributes in selection of Mate-Partners 95
7.11 Family Type and the Practice of allowing Boys to see the Mate before Marriage 98
7.12 Family Type and Permissiveness to Divorce 99
8.1 (a) Deviation from Role Conventionality with regard to Handling of Money related to Family Type and Caste 103
8.1 (b) Deviation from Role Conventionality in Families of Different Compositions and Economic Statuses 103
8.2 (a) Castewise Percentage of the Joint Families where Husband and Wife do not talk to each other freely 104
8.2 (b) Classwise Classification of the Joint Families where Husband and Wife cannot talk freely with each other 104
8.3 (a) Caste and Type of Families where Women are Final Decision maker with regard to Selection of Bride 105

8.3 (b)	Economic Status and Type of Families where Women are Final Decision-making Centres with regard to Selection of Birds	106
8.4 (a)	Caste, Family Type and Preferences for Employment over Education	106
8.4 (b)	Class, Family Type and Preference for Employment over Education	107
8.5 (a)	Caste, Family Type and the Practice of Matching Horoscopes	108
8.5 (b)	Economic Status, Family Type and Practice of Matching Horoscopes	109
8.6 (a)	Caste, Family Type and Preference for Love Match over arranged Marriage	109
8.6 (b)	Economic Status, Family Type and Preference for Love Match	110
8.7 (a)	Caste and the Type of Families where the Bridegrooms fully Participate in the Selection of Bride	110
8.7 (b)	Economic Status and the Type of the Families where the Bridegroom fully participates in the Selection of Bride	111
8.8 (a)	Caste, Family Type and Acceptance of Co-education	111
8.8 (b)	Economic Status, Family Types and Acceptance of Co-education	112
9.1	Family Type and Attitude towards Girl's Education	117
9.2	Level of Aspiration and Family Type	118
9.3	Attitude towards Education Family Type and Respondents' Education	119
9.4	Family, Type, Education of Respondents and Levels of Aspirations for Males	120
9.5	Family Type, Education of Respondents and Levels of Aspirations for Females	121
9.6	Education of the Head and the Attitude and Dimensions of the Respondents and Behavioural of Different Types of the Family	122

Preface

THE STUDY of the Hindu social system holds a great challenge for sociologists in India. The three essential units of this social system are: the family, the village and the caste. Although the village and the caste have received adequate attention at the hands of Indian and foreign sociologists, the family still needs a great deal of research, both in depth and in coverage.

Barring certain outstanding recent works, viz., the studies by Aileen D. Ross, Desai, Gore and Madan, the entire country is almost a *terra incognita* in the sphere of family studies. While Ross analyses the internal processes in the family and the areas of strain and stress generated by change in the structure of the society, Gore has studied the impact of urbanization upon the family by employing the structural functional approach. Desai, on the other hand, proposes a functional classification of family and has delved deep into the analysis of the pattern of mutual aid and observance of familial obligations by family members. Madan analyses the family pattern of Kashmiri Pandits. Thus, it appears that though all these works have contributed to our understanding of this basic institution, considerable work remains to be done to arrive at scientific formulations on the Hindu family.

The present work is a modest effort to supplement the existing literature on family in a hitherto unknown area with a view to providing comparative data on the Hindu family upon which ultimately theoretical formulations might be based.

The prime objective of the study has been to analyse the structure and internal processes of 160 families in Patna. Attempts have been made to have a comparison of the patterns revealed with regard to nuclear and joint families. This does not, however, mean that differences revealed are absolute. Any family structure is subject to various and quick changes and if a family changes its structure from joint to nuclear or vice versa it might not always depict any distinct pattern of behaviour immediately. Yet we should not forget that at any one point of time a family structure is a social reality and an analysis such as mine is capable of yielding fruitful results. Besides the structure of the family, economic status, caste of the family and education of the heads of the families have been taken as independent variables.

The work could not have been completed without the sympathetic and encouraging assistance of Dr. Sachchidananda, retired Professor of Sociology, A. N. Sinha Institute of Social Studies, Patna, under whose guidance the present work has been done. I am under debt of deep gratitude to him for his valuable suggestions, criticism, interest and insight on the subject.

I am thankful to my respondents who have extended their whole hearted cooperation in furnishing information on some of the inner most recesses of family life.

I shall be failing in my duty if I do not acknowledge my deep gratitude to my wife Manju Sinha who helped me by providing moral as well as academic support in the completion of the work. I am also thankful to Shri Naurang Rai of the Concept Publishing Company for his promptness in getting the work published. The manuscript has been typed by Shri K. N. Tiwary of the Sulabh International Centre for Action Sociology, Training and Rural Development. I am grateful to him for his contribution.

I am also thankful to my friends in the A. N. Sinha Institute of Social Studies and elsewhere for their sincere help in various ways.

AWADHESH KUMAR LAL

1

Introduction

THE FAMILY is a primary social institution, important to the individual and society. It is a social unit of which each one of us is a member. The family is in fact "the institution to which we owe our humanity" (Mead, 1953:4). It is the most remarkable of all our social institutions and is one of the oldest of human institutions. In fact "of all the organizations, large or small, which society unfolds, none transcends the family in the intensity of its sociological significance. It influences the whole life of society in innumerable ways and its changes reverberate through the whole social structure. It is capable of endless variations and yet reveals a remarkable continuity and persistence through change" (MacIver, 1949:330). Continuation and perpetuation of society through reproduction, social placement, protection and socialization are the universal functions of the family. In addition to these the family performs important economic, social control, educational, recreational and religious functions.

It is a social institution and structural arrangement for carrying out certain functions necessary for the continuity of society and maintenance of social order. It is called the "cradle of human nature". This is because it is the first place where the individual is socialized. It is the conduct through which initial status, basic skills and models of performance pass from one generation to another. As the repository of tradition, it acts as the transmission belt linking the past to the future (Goode, 1967). The family is the formative cell for continuing and perpetuating the way of life. For inculcating in its youth the traits of cultural values there has not been any substitute for family. Not only in modern sociological writings, but in ancient philosophical postulations also the importance and indispensability of the family have been noted. Social reformers and writers have all realized the importance of the family. That they were aware of the importance of family as the basic organ of society has been appropriately summarized in the following lines:

> "Philosophers and social analysts have noted that society is a structure made up of families and that the peculiarities of a given society can be described by outlining its family relations. The earliest moral and ethical writings suggest that a society loses its strength if people fail in their family obligations. Confucius thought, for example, that happiness and prosperity would prevail in the society if only everyone would behave 'correctly' as a family member which primarily meant that no one should fail in his filial obligations. The relationship between a ruler and his subjects, then, was parallel to that of a father and his children. Similarly, much of the early Hebrew writing, in Exodus, Deuteronomy Ecclesiastes, Psalms and Proverbs, is devoted to the importance of obeying family rules. In India, too, the earliest codified literature (the Rigveda about the last half of the second millennium B.C. and the law of Manu about the beginning of the Christian era) devotes great attention to the family" (Goode, 1965 : 1-2).

The study of the Hindu social system necessitates the study of the family. "Three things are absolutely necessary for the understanding of any cultural phenomenon in India. These are the configuration of the linguistic regions, the institution of caste and family organization. Each of these three together gives meaning and supplies the basis to all other aspects of Indian culture" (Karve, 1953 : 1)

Family Studies in India

Writers on religion, ethics, philosophy, law, as well as social research have contributed a great deal on the family. Now there exists "a vast literature on the family running all the way from superstition-based folklore to imaginative fiction, to poetic outpourings, to philosophical speculations, to popularized magazine articles and advice columns and, finally, to reports of scientific investigation" (Christensen, 1964: 3). However, before scientific research, interpretation of the family was highly speculative and emotional in nature. The work on family was then characterized by speculation and emotion.

According to Komarovsky and Waller (1945), interest in the

family became empirically and statistically oriented for the first time in the period ranging between 1915-1926. It was during this period that the family was viewed, for the first time, by the searchlight of science and research and by 1950, "and probably much before, it was proper to speak of the scientific study of marriage and the family" (Christensen, *op. cit.* : 9).

So far as research on the Indian family is concerned, family has been next only to caste in receiving the attention of the sociologists and considerable empirical research on family has been conducted during the last 25 years (Dube, 1971). Apart from the books especially dealing with the institution of family many studies on Indian villages and ethnographic studies contain, though in a limited perspective, certain dimensions of the institution of family. All these have contributed a great deal in providing meaningful comparative data to test various theories concerning the family. In this chapter, we propose to review certain works dealing exhaustively with the institution of family. This will enable us to have an idea of the variety of research conducted in this sphere including the dimensions covered in them. The factual evidences contained in them will be used as meaningful comparative data for our study.

In the first place, there is the study by Aileen D. Ross of the institution of family in an urban setting. This is a study of 157 families of Bangalore. The family has been studied in an urban setting because it is presumed that city people are more susceptible to Western influence, making the agents of change quite active. The respondents for the study belong to a number of castes but the majority among them are Brahmins. The respondents are from middle and upper-middle income groups and are mostly youngsters. In order to have cross-caste and cross-generational comparisons, persons from other castes and from older age groups have also been included in the sample survey. The respondents have been selected on the basis of convenience sampling, their responses have been recorded through structured interview. The aim of the study is to show how the traditional form of the joint family is changing its "structure and relations" under the pressure of forces like urbanization and industrialization.

The study reveals that the small joint family is the most popular form of family among the castes covered. The women appear to be more inclined to lead their life in the nuclear family. The younger generation appears to be less attached to their distant relatives than the older generations. Expectation of obligations also gets changed under the impact of urbanization. The power of the family is declining and intra-familial clashes are frequent. The husband-wife relationship is becoming closer. The traditional values attached to certain types of occupations are changing. A change from inherited or ascribed status to achieved status is giving birth to strain and stresses. The nuclear family appears to be more receptive to new trends in education, particularly girl's education.

The study shows that the attitudes of young men and women have been found to be more liberal in breaking caste endogamy. Changes are also found in other traditional marriage patterns. There might be several shortcomings in this study. But there are certain very good points also. "The originality of the study lies in its attempt to classify the many changes in responsibility, authority and affection which affect family relationships when structural changes occur" (Sachchidananda, 1961 : 249).

There is a study of the families of some Syrian Christians of Kerala by Kurian. The responses have been collected with the help of mailed questionnaires and in all 60 respondents from urban areas and 65 respondents from rural areas returned the completed questionnaires. All the respondents are well educated and are in the Rs. 500 or above monthly income bracket. The author has tried to study the families of these 125 respondents, with reference to family compositions, desirability of nuclear family, freedom in the choice of mate, acceptance of dowry, attitudes towards divorce, family planning, position of women and authority of parents over their children.

The author finds that on the whole respondents are relying less and less on tradition as a channel of culture transmission. The trend appears to be in favour of general changes in society. But the changes, according to the author, are not equally strong with regard to all items studied. The main emphasis of the book has been on a comparison between the responses of rural groups and those of urban groups. This shows that both the groups of the respondents favour mostly nuclear type of family, both are dead against even to the idea of divorce, both are not very authoritarian in dealing with their children. But in many cases the rural-urban variations become quite significant. In the case of composition of families, the urban respondents are mostly characterized by nuclear families and are more keen to accept family planning than the rural respondents. Similarly, the respondents from rural groups are in majority regular church-goers, prefer in larger proportion to confine women to household duties, prefer some type of restriction on mate choice by spouses in a larger degree than the urban families. The author, therefore, concludes that, in all, the urban families are more progressive than the rural families.

Then there is a study of family by I. P. Desai. This is a study of the family in Mahuva, a small town 60 miles south of Bhavnagar. In all, 425 households have been studied. The author has tried to deal with the jointness and nuclearity of the families. The extent of jointness is determined first on the basis of number of generations of lineal descendants living in a household. In the second part, the analysis of jointness has been made on the basis of kinship composition, ownership of property and mutual obligations. On the basis of these three indices, the author has proposed five types of families.

1. *Nuclear household with zero degree of jointness:* Those households which are nuclear in composition and have no relations or obligations with outside kin.
2. *Nuclear household with low degree of jointness:* Those nuclear households which have mutual obligations with outside kin but do not share any joint property.
3. *Nuclear household with high degree of jointness:* Those nuclear households which have relations of mutual obligations with outside kin having a share in property also.
4. *"Marginal" joint family*: Here marginality refers only to residential jointness. A marginal joint family has been defined to be a family where any addition or subtraction of a member would change the type.
5. *Traditional joint family*: There are households where three or more generations are living together in the same household, sharing property and fulfilling all obligations.

According to the findings, nearly 96 per cent of the families in Mahuva have some kind of jointness. Caste and religion do not appear to be significantly related with jointness. Jointness does not appear to be associated with any particular religion or caste group. It is found that there is lesser jointness among persons engaged in modern occupations as compared to persons engaged in agriculture or business. Longer stay in urban areas is not limited to jointness.

In Madan's work on kinship of Kashmiri Pandits, we find an analysis of family and kinship in the village Uttarsu Umangiri. It is based on one year's intensive and extensive field-work in the village.

Since the author himself is a Kashmiri Pandit he was in an advantageous position to fully analyze the social and religious life of the Pandits.

Madan points out that three important kin groups among the Pandits are: *Chulah, Kotamb* and *Kol*. The smallest and most discrete is *Chulah*. In the structure and function of the *Chulah*, bonds of agnation are very important. The *Chulah* may vary in composition. There is a division of labour based on age and sex in the *Chulah, Kotamb*, on the other hand, is less important as compared to *Chulah*. Generally the *Kotamb* as a whole does not have common ownership rights or socio-economic or ritual obligations towards its members. The third, the *Kol*, is the widest exogamous category and never acts as a group. Through the Chulah and Kotamb the Pandits live their domestic life.

Madan finds that the kinship among the Pandits is very important for streamlining their social life, yet it does not have a wide range of application among them particularly in politico-jural functions. Economic activity is also "becoming increasingly disassociated from kinship...." (p. 222).

Gore's study is an attempt to see the impact of urbanization on the perception, attitudes and behaviour patterns of the family. Many dimensions of the family have been analyzed to locate the pattern and extent of changes. To point out clearly the trend of change coming under urbanization, data from urban, fringe and rural families have been gathered. Another characteristic feature about the design of this study is that the author has studied families belonging to only one community, the Agrawala community. This is, of course, as Goode mentions in the foreword of this book, *On a Methodological Innovation*.

Gore has pointed out that so far as the size of the family is concerned the difference between urban and rural families is not very large. However, in size the urban joint families are larger than the non-urban joint families and urban nuclear families are smaller than the non-urban nuclear families. In their mental orientations, however, the urban families showed greater inclination for the nuclear family than the rural families. In the area of decision-making, their appears to be no difference in the patterns revealed for different types of families. The urban family has been found to be less tradition-oriented than the rural families insofar as women's work role and status are concerned. In the sphere of marriage also urban families respond more to modernity than the rural families. In brief, the patterns of rural/urban differences suggest that the differences are small on questions of actual behaviour such as size and composition of family and decision-making, and larger on questions of age of marriage, inter-caste marriage, divorce and family preference (p. 228). So far as the fringe group is concerned the responses reveal that it does not operate as the middle point between the rural and urban families.

Summing up the discussion on these works on the Indian family, we may say that while Gore has studied the impact of urbanization upon the family life by employing the structural functional approach, Ross analyses the areas of strains and stresses as witnessed in the realm of power, inter-personal relationship and affection, with the change in the structure of the society. In the third place, Desai has studied the mutual aid, ownership of property, observance of familial obligations by family members. He has on the basis of certain indices proposed a functional classification of the family. Quite distinct to these is the work of Kurian who has mainly compared the responses of few urban and rural respondents. Finally, Madan's work is an anthropological account of kinship and family in a single caste group of a particular village. Thus, in their approach, method, selection of respondents, each work is different from the other. All have contributed a great deal by systematically exploring the family which remained empirically a *terra incognita* for a considerable period of time.

Objectives of the Present Study

Social scientists, from different branches, have shown lively interest in the study of family. Currently, those, interested in studying the changing social structure of developing nations find it but necessary to investigate family also. This applies even to India. "The changing family is of academic interest to many fields of inquiry in India. Family planners are interested in, among other topics, fertility potentials or attitudes, sociologists in social structure, anthropologists in kin and economists in labour utilization, etc., (Conklin, 1969: 1445). Even among the sociologists, different scholars have chosen different dimensions of family for their studies. In view of the impracticability of studying every aspect of family at one time, the dimensions intended to be studied are bound to be limited. Some restrictions must be placed in order to select for studying some important facets. After scanning through relevant literature we have selected certain aspects of family which have not been widely touched and explored. The broad objectives of the present study may, therefore, be listed as below:

- to delineate the compositional types of the family;
- to discern patterns of regulations governing day-to-day interactional pattern in the family;
- to delineate the pattern of task differentiation in the family;
- to delineate the pattern of power structure in the family;
- to explore inter relations between family and occupation;
- to find out the extent of permissiveness in the fields of education and certain allied phenomena; and
- to get people's views in regard to certain practices connected with marriage and to delineate recent trends of Hindu marriage.

The behavioural and normative contents of the family have been studied in the light of the above guidelines. The above mentioned dimensions together have been taken as the dependent variable. While studying the behavioural pattern in the families and the attitudinal dimensions of the respondents, the compositional form of the family is the most important independent variable. In other words, it is our primary endeavour to analyze the response variations in the context of the familial composition. Over and above this, the importance of income, education and caste, as independent variables, has been examined with regard to certain dimensions. An attempt (where possible) to compare the findings of the present work with those of other related works has been made to pinpoint the general trend of family change. Finally, against this background we have tried to analyze the incongruity between normative extrapolation and/or traditionally prevalent behaviour, on the one hand, and the delineated behavioural propensities and attitudinal dimensions on the other. This has provided us with an insight into the pattern of change in the family. We have also tried to locate the areas of strain and stress in the family and their implications on the internal processes in the family.

Hypotheses

The hypotheses to be tested in the present studies are as follows:

1. The basic hypothesis which we propose to test is that if urban and modern influences are affecting the family system, greater

change would be visible in the nuclear family than the joint family. Nuclear families would reveal individualistic traits in larger proportion than the joint families.

2. Since now class and caste do not coincide and since urbanization is basically against the caste system, the economic status should provide a significant dimension to alter behavioural pattern of the family. Since educated persons are supposed to be more prone to individualistic and modern trends, it is hypothesized that families with highly educated heads would reveal a pattern of responses characterized by inclination to modernity.

Selection of the Sample and Techniques of Data Collection

The reliability and validity of any generalization based on empirical research, to a considerable extent, depends on the method of selection of the respondent and the various tools employed in data collection. When we have to select a number of persons from a very large number, we have to consider the various methods for selection of a representative sample. For our purpose we have selected respondents on the basis of purposive stratification and by the use of quota sampling. From an earlier survey conducted on Patna town, we got a rough estimate of castewise break-up of the Hindu population. Table 1.1 gives the above data.

In the first place we decided to select respondents from four such castes who are traditionally regarded as upper castes. Next we decided to select respondents from three such castes who are called "middle range castes". Here the data in Table 1.1 proved to be of great use. On the basis of the numbers we selected three castes, namely, Kurmi, Ahir (Yadava) and Bania. Then we decided to select respondents from "untouchable" castes. True, from Table 1.1 we find that Pasi, Dusadh and Dhobi have each a numerical edge over the Chamar, we opted for the Chamar. The Chamars are also one of the numerically dominant among the untouchables. The difference in the population of these four castes is negligible. The Chamars were selected simply because of the fact that we easily located areas of their concentration in Patna town. This made our work slightly easier. Finally, we decided to select an equal number of respondents from each of the caste categories. From each caste, we interviewed 20 respondents. In other words, each of the eight castes enumerated above constituted a cell and from each cell 20 families were selected for the study. In total, 160 families were studied. Here, in accordance with our objective, we incorporated in our samples families of diverse economic status. We also tried to get our samples from different areas of Patna.

Table 1.1: Distribution of 1,000 Hindus according to Caste

Caste	*Population*
Kayastha	164
Brahmin	119
Kurmi	116
Ahir	98
Bania	92
Kahar	70
Rajput	64
Pasi	23
Chai	22
Dusadh	20
Dhobi	19
Teli	19
Chamar	18
Sonar	16
Hajam	15
Kumhar	14
Barhi	12
Kanu	9
Lohar	8
Thathera	6
Mehtar	5
Dhanuk	3
Dom	1
Bendhihar	1
Others	66
	1,000

Source: Report on the Demographic Sample Survey of Patna, 1955.

On the basis of a review of 456 studies published in the period between 1947 and 1956, Nye (1964) indicates that the techniques of data collection, questionnaire and interview have been dominating family research in recent years. Between the two, the former loses all the potentialities in the case of an illiterate respondent. Secondly, as Komarovsky and Waller *(op. cit.)* feel that the respondents feel it unethical on the part of the researcher to violate the sanctity by making it a subject of research. Similar is the case with other aspects of family behaviour. Penetrating anybody's niche of personal life is bound to create annoyance and resistance on the part of respondents. In order to collect data on family excellent rapport is required which might help uncover guarded personal information. Here the potentiality of questionnaire becomes doubtful. In fact, the interview, therefore, is "the more appropriate technique for revealing information about complex emotionally laden subjects or for probing beyond public attitudes to the more covert private sentiments" (Selltis 1965: 242). Over and above this, when the interview is the method for data collection, the interviewer is in a position to contract or expand his tool whenever he feels necessary. Even in a highly structured interview, after setting the subject for discussion with the fixed questions, the interviewer can go deep into the phenomenon by developing further links with the subject.

In the present study we have used interview as the most important tool for the collection of raw material. The interview schedule is a structured one. In the beginning we used a semi-structured interview schedule. This we used to test the wording of questions, to categorize the responses as far as possible and to finalize the structured interview schedule. In other words, the semi structured schedule has been pre-tested on a sub-sample and suitably revised to facilitate the work of data collection in the final stages. To penetrate deep into any facet of family life, the investigator has gone beyond the fixed questions and has tried to collect many cases to illustrate various points. Moreover, wherever, the investigator, was, allowed by the respondents to observe the affairs of the families, he has availed that opportunity to check and illustrate the data gathered through interviews. In a nutshell, evidences documented from these sources have been the basic raw material for this study. Finally, in formulating the interview schedule we have endeavoured to incorporate various dimensions, yet caution has been taken to see that the interview guide is not made unnecessarily lengthy.

Definitions

The term "family" is used daily in common parlance. "Most people know intuitively what they mean by the 'family'. They have known families throughout their lifetime and intuitive definitions are sufficient for everyday conversation and action" (Farber 1966 : 1). Separating the popular usage of this term from the academic usage, we can say that even the popular usage of this term is highly fuzzy, bewildering and complex. In common parlance the term family may mean many things. For example, citing the use of this term in Western societies, Harris (1969) has aptly illustrated the various meanings that may be imputed to this term.

However, for academic purposes one cannot rely upon the popular usage of the term. In order to subject family to a rigorous scientific analysis, social scientists are required to formulate a precise and distinct definition of family. But among the social scientists also the use of this term is indiscriminate. To quote Prabhu (1964 : 204):

> "Though almost everybody is born in a family and seems to know and understand what family is from first-hand experience, yet the many special studies which have been devoted in recent years to 'the family' bring out very prominently how very difficult it is to define precisely and briefly the institution of family".

Different social scientists have defined the family differently, each according to his own point of view. "Even anthropologists and sociologists, both interested in social structure, differ markedly in their definitions, a difference which makes it very difficult to relate data from anthropological studies of families living in pre-industrial societies to sociological data collected after these families move to the city" (Ross, 1961: 29). Coming nearer to sociology, we find that here also there is lack of unanimity over the definition of the family. "Sociologists have developed several interpretative approaches to variations in family life, each one generating unique understanding about family organization, while at the same time emphasizing a different aspect. These variations in emphasis result in slightly modified definitions of the family in each approach" (Farber, *op. cit.*). "If we analyse the various definitions of family we find that commonly it is regarded as more or less closely integrated group of people who are related to one another through ties of kinship, blood or adoption" (Ross, *op. cit.*).

However, before we proceed further in the analysis of the problem of family, in order to get exactly the meaning and scope of inquiry, we must spell out what we mean by "family". After taking into consideration a number of definitions given by Indian sociologists we define family as follows:

> "Family is a group comprising at least one married couple living in a household and taking food cooked at a common hearth. Such persons should be related among themselves by blood, adoption or by other acknowledged generational relationship".

This is indeed a structural definition and consequently might be subjected to criticisms in a number of ways. For example, when Kapadia (1959) maintains that functionally a residential unit of husband, wife and their children might not constitute a nuclear family, it means that, according to him, the functional basis is more important than the structural unit. Secondly, such definitions are often said to exempt the effective kin group which the term family should imply (Lambert, 1963). In spite of the weakness, this definition has certain advantages and does not contain the weaknesses inherent in certain other definitions.

In the first place, taking the cue from Desai (1955) and Kapadia *(op. cit.)* if we define family as a constellation of certain functions, the question arises as to how to differentiate it 'from another social group which theoretically, at least, may possess the same constellation of functions? Such a definition would reduce observable regulations to a hodge podge and render the comparative method worthless '(Lynch, 1963: 187-88). Secondly, as Lambert *(op. cit.)* puts, if otherwise defined it might be difficult to define the outer edges of the family. In the third place adopting functional definition of Kapadia would mean that "all family systems in the major cultural areas of the world, including the West, become joint families" (Goode, 1968: 243). This would create puzzles. Then again even in those works emphasizing functional nuclearity (as in the case of 'some aspects of family in Mahuva') it becomes clear that residential units are of primary significance and it would be wrong to leave them unnoticed. To quote Abbi (1969: 51).

> "Desai's own informants conceived of nuclearity and jointness primarily in terms of residential nuclearity and 'joint residence' ...which shows that in their conception of family relations these facts are of greater significance than Desai would concede".

Except at two places in the chapter on "Size and Composition of the Family,"[1] in the entire work the term nuclear family includes, for our purpose, a residential unit consisting of husband, wife and their unmarried children with or without one or more separated, unmarried or widowed relatives.

The term "joint family" refers to a residential unit consisting of at least two married couples taking food cooked at a common hearth and where the married males are related with each other by blood, adoption, marriage or by other acknowledged genealogical links. It may include one or more separated unmarried or widowed relatives.

The term "head of the family" would imply the eldest male member of the family. In case he is not articulate it would mean the next eldest male.

Delimitation of the Study

India is a vast country and is divided into a number of groups and subgroups. Even in a small town like Patna there are many religious groups. For all of them, a single line of change cannot be postulated. As such we have concentrated upon only one religious group. The findings regarding the family are applicable to the Hindu families within the jurisdiction of the Patna Municipal Corporation.

In the second place, the detailed findings of this work are applicable, by and large, to the families concerned in this study. The tables of statistics appended to the study should be looked as summations of the interview material rather than valid statistical generalizations.

We agree with the view that: "At one point of time, the size and actual composition of a family often denotes a particular stage in the development cycle. Simple families grow into extended families and then break up into simple families again" (Dube, 1963: 177). With birth and adoption the size of the family increases and with the marriage of any male in patrilineal society the simple (nuclear) household becomes an extended one. Similarly, by death, partition, etc., the compositional type of the household changes. From extended it may become nuclear. Of course, there might be certain pattern in the development process of the household but it is not cyclical in nature. This is to be kept in mind while analysing the attitudinal dimensions of the respondents. The attitudinal dimensions of the respondents might not always be influenced by the compositional type of family. If a person lives today in a joint family and few days after if his family becomes nuclear, there might not be any perceivable change in his attitudes. Attitudes and behaviour are fostered by a constellation of socio-economic and psychological variables.

While analysing the changes in family we have relied upon the description of these dimensions in traditional societies as put by authoritative writers. In these, there is always a danger that they might not have differentiated between the norms and their practice. "The publicly acknowledged values and ideals of the recent past can be gathered from literary, philosophical and religious sources, but we know neither how fully the 'average' Hindu accepted these ideals nor how well he followed them in practice" (Goode, *ibid.*, 203). Of course, we have tried to be greatly discriminating in selecting past data on the various dimensions of the family, yet there might be certain shortcomings in this regard. What have been written for the Hindu society as a whole might not be true for every strata of Hindu society.

Correlation of responses with one or more variables does not imply that other variables are not important.

The Town of Patna

Patna, the capital of Bihar, is the place where this study had been conducted. The town is situated on the right bank of the Ganga. According to the 1971 census it has a population of 4,73,572.[2] The Hindus are more than 80 per cent of the total population. Portraying the history and social profile of the town the census says:

> "Ruins of the ancient city of Patliputra have been found in Kumhrar. Patna city area developed in the 16th century, Bankipore area sprung up in the 18th and 19th centuries, while the new capital area was built in the last 50 years. Patna has many ancient sacred places and places of worship: the Bari and Chhoti Patan Devi for the Hindus, the Mausoleum at Sultanganj for Muslims, the Gurdwara in Patna City for Sikhs and the *Padri Ki Haveli* (a Roman Catholic Church built in 18th century) for Christians.
>
> "Patna lies on the main line of the Eastern Railway and is well connected by road. A regular steamer ferry service connects it to North Bihar.
>
> "Patna is mainly an administrative and educational centre. It is developing and new residential colonies are coming up fast, e.g., Rajendra Nagar, Shrikrishna Nagar, Shrikrishna Puri and Patliputra Colony" (1961, xi).

NOTES

1. In those places we have used nearly ten categories of families, in order to give a detailed description of the family types.
2. See *Commerce*, Vol. 123, No. 3144, 1971, p. 302.

2

SIZE AND COMPOSITION OF THE FAMILY

THE FORMS and composition of family are the most important analytical points in the study of residence, kinship terminology, marriage and any topic concerning the study of kinship and social organization. In any discussion on family the variations in organizational structures of the family have a number of implications for predictions in regard to it. Therefore, the analysis of the compositional forms of the family is a matter of analytical priority in any study of family. The composition of the family has a considerable influence in the shaping of actions and interactions in the routine operation of this institutional structure. It affects the pattern of intra-family interactions determining in major part the degree to which any two family members interact. By shaping the content of relationship within the family, the family type and varying composition of families determine, in part, the pattern of strained adjustment among relatives. Socialization patterns and economic exchanges are also partly determined by the forms of the family. In Hindu society, for example, in a multi-generational family, the mother-in-law in several cases supervises the socialization of the daughter-in-law, which is not common in the Western nuclear family. Pinpointing the influences of a polygynous and a nuclear household on the socialization of a child, Goode (1965) maintains that a young child in a polygynous household sees "a wider range of adult models intimately than he could observe in a nuclear family". Since the interactional patterns of diverse compositional forms differ, the family type is likely to affect the structure of authority and the pattern of role performance in the family. For example, in traditional joint families the oldest male is the 'pinnacle' of the hierarchy and the responsibilities of earning bread are diffused on all able-bodied members, whereas the head of the nuclear family has to bear the heavy burden of responsibility alone and has to take all decisions himself without the help of other kinsmen (Ross, 1961). Thus the analysis of the internal processes in the family necessitates an analysis of the compositional form of the family. In this chapter we present an analytical sketch of the compositional form of the family with a view to delineating the different types of urban families and their relationships with such variables as caste, income, education, numerical composition and age of the head of the family in order to see their influence, if any, on the distribution of the types of urban families.

Scheme for Classification

Here a description of the different family categories used in this chapter would not be out of place. In the study of Indian families a number of family classifications have been used. Kolenda (1968:346-47) on the basis of 26 family studies has proposed a number of compositional categories. A detailed enumeration of these categories in the words of the author herself is given below:

1. *Nuclear Family*: A couple with or without unmarried children.
2. *Supplemented Nuclear Family*: A nuclear family plus one or more unmarried, separated or widowed relatives of the parents other than their unmarried children.
3. *Sub-Nuclear Family*: A fragment of a nuclear family. Typical examples are the widow with unmarried children or siblings–whether unmarried or widowed, separated or divorced–living together.
4. *Single-person Household*
5. *Supplemented Sub-nuclear*: A group of relatives, members of a formerly complete nuclear family, plus some other unmarried, divorced or widowed relative who was not a member of the nuclear family. For example, a widow and her unmarried children plus widowed mother-in-law.
6. *Collateral Joint Family*: Two or more married couples between whom there is a sibling bond, usually a brother-brother relationship plus unmarried children.
7. *Supplemented Collateral Joint Family*: A collateral joint family plus unmarried, divorced or widowed relatives. Typically such supplemental relatives are the widowed mother of the married brothers or the widower father or an unmarried sibling.

8. *Lineal Joint Family*: Two couples between whom there is a lineal link, usually between parents and married son, sometimes between parents and married daughter.
9. *Supplemented Lineal Joint Family*: A lineal joint family plus unmarried, divorced or widowed relatives who do not belong to either of the lineally linked nuclear families, e.g., the father's widower brother or the daughter-in-law's unmarried brother.
10. *Lineal Collateral Joint Family*: Three or more couples linked lineally and collaterally. Typically, parents and their two or more married sons plus the unmarried children of the three or more couples.
11. *Supplemented Lineal-collateral Joint Family*: A lineal collateral joint family plus unmarried, widowed, separated relatives who belong to none of the nuclear families lineally and collaterally linked, e.g., the father's widowed sister or brother or an unmarried nephew of the father.
12. *Others.....*

We have also adopted the same scheme of family classification in this chapter. This is, first, because of the fact that these categories have been worked out after a thorough analysis of 26 studies dealing with family classification. Secondly, each of these categories is descriptive of its contents and from "a title it is possible to imagine accurately the composition of the families included" (*ibid.* : 349). Thirdly, this scheme of classification is quite exhaustive and the categories are mutually exclusive.

Compositional Types of the Families

One of the consequences expected from the introduction of a money economy and from urbanization is the dissolution of the joint family. While Parsons (1961) observes: "A historic trend to whittle down the size of kinship units in the general direction of isolating the nuclear family", Burgess and Locke (1953) point out that industrialization and urbanization lead to transformation of the institutional family towards companionship family. Nimkoff (1959) also holds that economic changes are bound to create change in family life. Similar observations have been made by Weber (1950), Writh (1938), Ross (*op. cit.*) and others. In sum, all these emphasize that there is close inverse relation between urbanization and industrialization on the one hand and the extended family on the other. The new modes of livelihood generated by urbanization offer differential opportunities to members of the same joint family. High social and geographical mobility created by urbanization often makes it necessary for brothers and sons to live away from each other in their separate places of work resulting in smaller families having changed composition. The value of orientation and ways of life produced by urbanization, manifesting themselves in individualization of attitudes and values, result in an increase in the number of nuclear families. The analysis of the data collected for the present study also reveals the preponderance of nuclear families (71%) over the joint families (29%).

The classification of the families into various compositional types (Table 2.1), categorized according to the types of extension by kin categories, reveals that traditionally bound value orientations will play a significant role in the sense that the nuclear families are not completely isolated and independent.

Table 2.1 : Distribution of Families into Different Compositional categories

Family Type	*% of Families*
1. Nuclear	46.3
2. Supplemented Nuclear	25.0
3. Collateral Joint	2.5
4. Supplemented Collateral Joint	3.1
5. Lineal Joint	11.2
6. Supplemented Lineal Joint	3.8
7. Lineal Collateral Joint	7.5
8. Supplemented Lineal Collateral Joint	0.6

As much as 36.2 per cent of the nuclear families are supplemented nuclear families. The nature of the nuclear families is different from that of the nuclear families of a society characterized by extreme industrialization. An analysis of the various types of the joint families, reveals that among the joint families, the ordering of relationship is, in a majority of cases, lineal rather than lateral. This points out the possibility that after the death of the father the normal amount of amity between the families of brothers disappears and there is a separation in the family.

Caste and Family Types

After the classification of the families, it is now proposed to explore the relationship between family types and caste. Putting the eight castes studies under two broad categories of upper caste Hindus (comprising Brahmins, Rajputs, Kayasthas, Bhumihars) and lower caste Hindus (comprising Kurmis, Yadavas, Baniyas, Chamars), the cross-tabulation of caste with family types shows that in the two caste groups the distribution of nuclear and joint families is exactly the same. The proposition that the joint family is a characteristic of the upper castes is not supported by our study. On the contrary the study postulates that caste is not an important determinant of family types. Though the difference in caste values and caste statuses does not seem to be related to the family types among the upper and lower castes, yet Table 2.2 shows that the percentage of supplemented nuclear family is higher in upper castes when compared to the percentage of supplemented nuclear families in lower castes.

Table 2.2 : Family types among upper and lower castes

	Family type	*Upper Caste percentage*	*Lower Caste percentage*
1.	Nuclear	40.0	52.5
2.	Supplemented Nuclear	31.2	18.8
3.	Collateral Joint	2.5	2.5
4.	Supplemented Collateral Joint	3.8	2.5
5.	Lineal Joint	10.0	12.5
6.	Supplemented Lineal Joint	6.2	1.2
7.	Collateral Lineal Joint	5.0	10.0
8.	Supplemented Collateral Lineal Joint	1.3	0.0

This indicates that though the joint family as a phenomenon is not confined to the upper caste Hindus, yet the nuclear families of the upper caste Hindus possess in larger proportions the rudiments of the joint family in the form of supplemented nuclear families reflecting the persistence of old joint family norms among upper caste Hindus. On the other hand the nuclear families of the lower caste Hindus are structurally more nuclear than the upper-caste Hindus. The castewise distribution of the different forms of joint families does not present any significant feature.

Education and Family Types

Like caste, education is said to be an important variable inversely related with extended families. Education of a person is considered an important factor in the behavioural outlook of an individual. It is generally expected that people with high educational level differ in taste from those who remain under low educational status. "Education by instituting new values and attitudes, by developing new needs and wants, by providing the means of access and developing willingness in the individual to acquire and accept new experience cannot be a powerful agent of change" (Morrisson, 1959: 67). One may expect that persons with high education would largely prefer nuclear form of family and in practice also highly educated persons should be found having nuclear families of their own. With this aim in view a correlation between type of family and education of the head a household has been made.

The study shows that there is a highly significant association between familism and the various levels of educational attainment of the head of the families. In fact, there seems to be a positive relation between high education of the head of the family and the number of the nuclear family. The proportion of nuclear family increases as the educational level of the head of the family increases.

Table 2.3: Family types and educational attainments of the head of households

Educational Level	*Nuclear Family*	*Joint Family*
Illiterate	10.5	13.0
Below Matric	19.3	30.4
Matriculate	20.2	19.6
Above Matric	50.0	36.9

Majority of the heads of households of nuclear families are those who have some post-school education. In the case of the joint families there are very few heads of households who have high education (above matric). Thus, it suggests that there is a positive correlation between high education and nuclear family on the one hand, and inverse relation between high education and the percentage of joint families (Table 2.3).

Income and Family Types

Exploration of relation between the family type and economic status has revealed that joint families tend to appear in the upper and upper middle income groups (Morrisson : *op. cit*; Nimkoff : *op. cit.*; Ross: *op. cit.*). Mandelbaum (1959) says that it is the characteristic of "wealthier strata of society". The information collected confirms the postulation that economic status is an important determinant so far as family types are concerned. Table 2.4 shows that most of the families with extended kinship network are in high income groups with highest percentage in the highest income category. In the case of the nuclear families the majority of the families fall in the income group of Rs. 101 to 300 (per month). This is natural because, in urban life, the families with high income only can meet the needs and necessities of large families. Unless the income of the family is fairly high, sufficient income for urban living can be made available by the aggregation of the earnings of several heads of different subunits of the extended families which might not be the position in the case of nuclear families, particularly in a society where mostly families are engaged in non-remunerative household work.

Table 2.4 : Family types and monthly income of the families

Income group	*Family Type*	
	Nuclear %	*Joint* %
1. Families having monthly income of Rs 100 or below	4.4	4.4
2. Families having monthly income between Rs 101 and 300	56.1	26.1
3. Families having monthly income between Rs 301 and 500	21.9	19.6
4. Families having monthly income between Rs 501 and 800	11.4	21.7
5. Families having monthly income of Rs 801 or above	6.1	28.2

Age of the Heads and Family Types

The system maintenance of the joint family emphasizes great deference and respect to the aged. It should, therefore, be expected that, in the interest of the system maintenance of the joint family, the heads of the joint families must be fairly old persons.

Table 2.5 : Family types and age of the heads of the families

Age Groups	*Family Types*	
	Nuclear %	*Joint* %
25 years and below (very young)	7.9	2.2
Between 26 years and 40 years (young)	58.8	23.9
Between 41 and 60 years (middle-aged)	29.8	63.0
61 years and above (old)	3.5	10.9

Table 2.5 shows that most heads of joint families are old persons. It points out that even if the sons are there and even if they are earning, in the case of joint families old age is an important prerequisite for being the head of a joint family. The absence of fairly old heads of families in the case of nuclear families indicates that with the increase in the age of a person, the family might become joint in nature. Table 2.5 shows that in the majority of the nuclear families, heads are young or very young while in majority of the joint families heads are middle-aged or old.

Size of the Family and Family Types

After presenting the analysis of the compositional form of the family it is also necessary to find out the correlation between the family types and size of the family. A comparison of the mean household size of the nuclear (4.91) and joint families (8.36) reveals that the nuclear families are smaller than joint families. The data (see Table 2.6) also show that nuclear families are small and medium in the case of a large percentage of families, while the large proportions of joint families fall in the categories of large and medium families. It is also obvious that the largest proportion of families among the nuclear families are of small size. Thus with the discussion of the size of the family we may hypothesize that there is a significant relation between size and types of family. With certain exceptions large and very large families are expected to be joint in structure in most of the cases. But it is also apparent that there is considerable overlapping in the case of the medium-size families. Due to many factors the joint family in the majority of the cases appears to be of medium size and if there is a medium-size family, only on the basis of its size we cannot make even a guess of its type.

Table 2.6 : Size of the family and family types

	Size of the Family	*Family Type*	
		Nuclear %	*Joint* %
1.	Small (consisting of 2 to 5 members)	65.8	10.9
2.	Medium (consisting of 6 to 9 members)	32.4	60.8
3.	Large (consisting of 10 to 12 members)	1.8	19.6
4.	Very large (consisting of 13 or more members)	0.0	8.7

To sum up, then, in this chapter we have tried to delineate the different types of urban families and their relationships with certain variables as caste, income and numerical composition of the family, and education and age of the heads of the families. In the first place we found that among the families included in the sample, the nuclear families are in larger percentage than the joint family. However, we also found that a number of nuclear families are supplemented in nature. Secondly, the proposition that the joint family is a characteristic of the upper castes is not supported by our study. In fact caste did not figure as an important variable in this case. Thirdly, there was a positive correlation between high education and nuclearization of the family. Fourthly, there was also a positive correlation between high income and the joint type of family. Fifthly, the joint family is headed by old or middle aged persons and in the nuclear families the heads are mostly very young or young. Lastly, we found that majority of the large and very large families are no doubt joint families, yet the joint families themselves are found to be of medium size in a majority of the cases. Thus the size and size alone of the family cannot decide the type of the family.

3

DIVISION OF LABOUR IN THE FAMILY

THERE are strong cross-cultural regularities in the patterning of task-differentiation between males and females. Some tasks are generally allocated to men while others are generally performed by women. Men are stronger and are, therefore, assigned hard work outside the house; and women, because of their being handicapped at times by pregnancy and menstruation and due to their child-rearing function, take over the household duties. However, very little of this division of labour is required only by the biological peculiarities of the two sexes (Goode, 1965). In fact women have enough strength to perform all tasks in every society. Secondly, what is defined as man's job in one society may become woman's job in another. This indicates that by and large the tasks of men and women are set to some extent by custom or are based on a number of factors in which the biological factor is only a part. Whatever may be the reasons, in no society are men and women free to choose whatever tasks they want using the criteria of efficiency, convenience and capacity. In each society there are verbalized norms which label some tasks as "feminine" while others as "masculine". But adherence to these norms is by no means universal.

Basing our discussion on the level of verbalized norms we can bring into focus the tasks which are masculine and those which are feminine in the Hindu society. Like most countries, among the Hindu families of India men earn to support the family. Besides the occupational role, men also have to take responsibility for community contacts, a major portion of which is devoted to negotiations relating to marriage in the family (Gore, 1968). They must also assert their superiority on the family scene by being able to control and keep under discipline the women and children of the family. On the other hand since taking up any role or function which is culturally defined as feminine will bring only social scorn and ridicule on them, they have to leave women relatively free in their own sphere (Dube, 1963).

While men earn, women take care of the home. They find their major responsibilities in the preparation of food, care of children, and all the washing, scrubbing, cleaning and sweeping involved in the care of a home. Earning and giving economic support to the family are not her primary responsibilities, she undertakes them only if she has to and she has the sympathy of the community with her (Gore, *ibid.*; Dube, *ibid.*).

After briefly sketching the tasks of men and women in a family on the basis of the verbalized norms, against this background, let us examine the sex-patterning of tasks in the families as well as latitude for exceptions in sex-typed tasks correlating the latter with the difference in the composition of the families representing different social environment. Afterwards, we will attempt a detailed analysis of the division of labour in the joint family.

From the behavioural field[1] of family we chose 10 tasks which are performed by members of a family in day-to-day life. These tasks fall under three important regions of the behavioural field of the family, viz.:

1. Economic activities;
2. Child care and control; and
3. Household duties.

Three items are taken to represent the activities in the economic field, four representing activities in the field of child care and control while the remaining three items represent activities in the field of household duties. In fact, by examining the pattern of performance of these activities, we will analyse the observance of role-conventionality[2] by families of different types.

The pattern of performance of the three activities concerning economic duties of the family indicates that these are the prime province of the male in both the nuclear and joint families. The variation in the strictness in observance of role-conventionality in the above activities may be attributed to the forces of industrialization and urbanization which produce a milieu different from the traditional one. Opening of numerous shops for all types of goods, necessity of purchasing every thing for daily consumption, cash payment for the purchases on the one hand and busy daily life of males in the city on the other, in some cases, make it essential and in some cases very helpful to males. But it is also apparent that women in only a few cases have removed the traditional barrier against going out for shopping on their own. In the discharge of the above duties, differences in family composition do not make any significant change (Table 3.1).

Table 3.1 : Family types and performance of economic duties by females or by males and females together

	Name of the Activity	*Types of Family*	
		Nuclear %	*Joint* %
1.	Handling of money	14.9	15.2
2.	Purchase of vegetables	20.6	16.7
3.	Purchase of clothes for children	24.5	22.7

Analysing the pattern of performance of the activities in the field of child care and control, it may be mentioned that traditionally the female has the chief responsibility for the care and training of the child. The data represented by Table 3.2 reveal that so far as washing, feeding and telling stories to the children are concerned, they remain primarily the domains of the females. So far as teaching children at home is concerned this is primarily the responsibility of the male. The distribution of data by family types shows that women from nuclear families are more likely to be helped by men in washing, feeding and telling stories to their children than women from the joint families. This may be explained by the fact that the nuclear family is a very tight unit comprising very few persons and when the woman is the lone member to look after the children, she can find help mainly from her husband. On the other hand, in the joint family the grandmother and other women may help her in the training and care of the children. In the case of teaching children at home, we find that the extent of latitude for exceptions is larger in the nuclear family than the joint family with the larger proportion of women helping men in the activity. This may again be attributed to the existence of either no or small number of relatives who may share the responsibility.

In the region of household duties we have selected three activities, viz., cooking, washing dishes and dusting and the pattern of performance of these activities reveals a pattern characterized by female's exclusiveness and autonomy. While analysing the conduct of activities in the field of child care and economic duties, we found that the pattern of task-performance in these fields also follows a particular sex-pattern but, within these broad limits, there was a significant difference in both types of family. In the case of household duties, however, there is no departure from the conventional pattern of performance. So far as the household duties are concerned the sex segregation is very rigid. This is primarily due to the fact that the social norms in the Hindu family are so strong that any participation in these activities makes a man an object of ridicule.

Table 3.2 : **Responsibility of child care and its performance by various types of the families**

	Name of the Activities	*Percentage of cases where the activities are performed by males or by males and females together.*	
		Nuclear Family	*Joint Family*
1.	Bathing of the children	12.9	3.5
2.	Feeding the children	11.8	3.5
3.	Telling stories to the children	21.8	30.7
4.	Teaching the children at home	53.1	76.3

In the pattern of performance of different activities from different behavioural fields in the family, so far as degree of exceptions in sex-typed tasks is concerned, we find that on one extreme certain household duties are the province of women and there is a strict division of labour. At the other extreme are the fields of child care and economic activities, where there is lesser segregation between men and women. Analysing the extent of variation from the conventional pattern of performance we find that in those regions, which are the domain of men, the degree of variation is greater when compared to the degree of variation in the activities by women. That is to say, the fear of being unconventional and existence of social opprobrium is strong in the case of men sharing women's work. Particularly in the case of the joint family, the existence of deterrent against participating in women's work is clearly more marked when compared with that of the nuclear family. In other words the joint family observes more segregation between men and women in the activities dominated by women than the nuclear family.

After the analysis of the pattern of role-conventionality observance by different types of family with regard to certain activities from these regions of the behavioural field of family, we know switch over to a detailed analysis of the division of labour in the joint family. In the nuclear family the husband and wife are the pivot around whom the family revolves. A description of the pattern of performance of different activities sexwise may illustrate to a great extent the division of labour in the family, so far as these activities are concerned. On the other hand in the case of the joint family, the existence of more than one family of procreation necessitates a further detailed description of allocation of various responsibilities of different members of the family. Since the joint family is not supposed to encourage a sense of individualism and emphasis on conjugal roles, we, by the analysis of division of labour in the joint family, may see how far the pattern of task performance delineated by the study is either conducive to the maintenance of the joint family or speaks of the potential sources of break or tension in the joint family.

To start with the economic activities (Table 3.3(a), (b)), handling of money for household expenses seems to be an exclusive preserve of the heads of the families or their wives. In all, except one joint family, the different nuclear families, combined to form the joint family, do not manage the household expenses individually for their own family of procreation. As one respondent observed:

> "My sons were earning and I was responsible for the household expenses. As such to meet the expenses once I took some loan, and although the loan was taken to meet the expenses of the entire family, my sons refused to help. Somehow or the other when the loan was paid, I directed my sons to pay the household expenses themselves, so far as their families are concerned".

In another case though the responsibility of handling money for household expenses was of the head, the taking of a job by his son created a problem for his family. As a respondent observed:

> "When my eldest son took up a job, it was expected that he would contribute at least something for the family too. Several months passed, but he did not think it to be his responsibility to contribute even slightly in the family purse. Consequently I took a stern decision. I asked him to henceforth look after the expenses of his own

wife and children or leave the house. The formula worked and now he contributes at least so much that I can manage for the entire family".

Table 3.3 (a) : Economic activities in the Joint Family

Task Performer	Name of the activities	
	Handling of money for household expenses	*Purchase of vegetables*
1. Eldest male who is simultaneously the head of the family	37	32
2. Eldest female who is also wife of the head of the family	6	5
3. Head of the family, his wife and any other member together	-	1
4. Each head for his own family of procreation	1	0
5. Eldest female other than wife of the head	1	1
6. Servants	0	4
7. Children	0	3
8. Others : Males	1	0
Females	0	0

However, in no case handling of money for household expenses is the privilege of a junior bride in the joint family. In one supplemented collateral joint family assigning household expenses by the widow mother of the brothers proved to be very conducive to the maintenance of peace in the family. In the words of a respondent:

"There might be differences between brothers, but so long as they have confidence, in one individual, the chances for strains are little. As, for example, handling of household expenditure by my mother has left little chance for any possible strain in my or my brother's family of procreation".

Table 3.3 (b) : Economic activities in the Joint Family

Task Performer		*Name of the Activity Purchase of clothes for children*
1. Eldest male who is also head of the family	(a) When he purchases for his own children only	15
	(b) When he purchases for other's children	10
2. Eldest female who is also head of the family	(a) When she purchases for her own children only	4
	(b) When she purchases for other's children	3
3. Each head for his own family of procreation		6
4. Wife of the head of (for her own children) each family of procreation		1
5. Each husband and wife (for their own children)		1
6. Head of the family and his wife (for their own children)		1
7. Eldest female who is not head of the family (for the children of others)		1
8. Others: Male		3
Female		0
9. Not applicable		–

From Table 3.3(a) it is apparent that the same pattern of division of labour operates in the purchase of vegetables except that we find that in certain cases vegetables are purchased through children and servants. But in the case of purchase of clothes for children [Table 3.3 (b)] in the family, the pattern of task-performance changes considerably as in a large number of joint families the individualistic pattern supposed to be prevalent in nuclear families gets an overt expression. Such tendencies are bound to create strains highly inimical to the existence of the joint family system. A case from a joint family is given below:

> "I have great affection for children of my elder brother. In fact they receive affection from all members. But now my elder brother does not listen to our needs. If he has to purchase clothes, he will purchase for his children, himself and wife but not for his younger brothers. I know the day our parents die, we would not live with him. In a family like ours, he has shown a tendency which is very selfish and naturally everybody will follow his course."

However, from Table 3.3(b) it is also clear that apart from purchasing for their own sons, the heads, in a significant number of cases, are responsible for the purchase of clothes for children of others also. The tendency of nuclearization or individualization by different units becomes widely manifest in the region of child care when we say that children in many cases are being looked after by their mothers. In those cases where child care is the responsibility of those other than the mother of the child, cooperation of ladies for sharing this responsibility is also marked [Table 3.4(a)]. So far as story-telling is concerned, out of 26 families where stories are told to children, majority remains the concern of the head of the family or his wife. This is due to the factor of age and experience. But there also in a good number of cases an individual family unit is responsible for this. This is also the point so far as the case of the activity of teaching children at home is concerned. In many cases this appears to be the prime duty of the child's parents [Table 3.4(b)].

Table 3.4 (a) : Carrying on the responsibility of child-care in the Joint Family

Task Performer	*Name of Activities*	
	Washing children	*Feeding children*
1. Each mother to her child/ children	11	11
2. Wife of the head of the family	8	8
3. All women jointly	9	9
4. Wife of the head of the family and the head of the family himself	1	0
5. Head of the family	0	1
6. Not applicable	17	17

In the case of household duties, however, it appears that in nearly all the cases it was pointed out that the responsibility is shared by all females. When asked about the primary responsibility for cooking, 24 families named wife of the head of the family. In three cases it was eldest daughter-in-law. In the rest all females together look after cooking. Approximately the same pattern prevails in the case of dusting and washing utensils, with the only exception that, in families which have the facility, this remains the duty of servants and maid-servants.

Table 3.4(b) : Carrying on the responsibility of child care in the joint family

Task Performer	*Name of the Activities*	
	Story telling to the children	*Teaching children at home*
1. Mother of the child/ children	7	3
2. Father of the child/ children	0	7
3. Parents of the child/ children jointly	1	0
4. Head of the family and the eldest male	5	8
5. Wife of the head of the family	9	2
6. Head of the family and his wife jointly	2	0
7. All females together	2	0
8. Others	0	1
9. Not applicable	20	25

In brief, in this chapter we have tried to study, first, the extent of observance of role-conventionality by the different types of families in the light of the 10 activities representing the fields of economic duties, child care and household duties. In this connection we found that, in the last two fields, there is lesser segregation between males and females in task performance. We also found that the sharing of women's part of work by male is less frequent than the sharing of men's work by females. We also found that the joint family maintains more strict control over men's and women's tasks in the activities dominated by females than the nuclear family. Secondly, we attempted a detailed analysis of division of labour in the joint family. Here we found that the respect for age and authority is more marked in the field of economic duties, but due to many factors of change, in other cases, the tendency to individualism is widely manifest.

NOTES

1. Herbst (1961) defines behavioural field of any individual/group as all those various activities that the individual/members of the group are found to engage in.
2. Role conventionality refers to men doing only traditional men's work and women doing traditional women's work (Hill, 1965).

4

INTER-PERSONAL RELATIONSHIP IN THE FAMILY

THE FAMILY is the main stable informal structure of the society. It is a web of relations between individuals or between, what Homans (1957 : 231) calls, "social personalities". These social personalities occupy different status and rank in the family unit. As such, the social roles of each family member can either be satisfying or a source of threat to the unity of the structure. For the successful operation of the family structures, therefore, the relationships among various members are built up and maintained through attitudes of fear, respect, obedience, avoidance as well as love. The role of relations internal to the family, that reflect the position of family members, is subject to norms and mores of the society, and in most of the societies patterns of interaction among members of the family depend upon the inter-play of age, sex and relationship roles.

Since a study on family change necessitates a study of changing inter-actional pattern in the family and to "a student of social change it might immediately be fruitful to look for changing attitudes and role definitions rather than change in the percentage of joint and nuclear households" (Gore; Desai, 1966:197). So in this chapter we propose to consider changing patterns of inter-personal relations of the members of the Hindu family. We have tried to delineate pattern of interactions between certain pairs of relationships. These are as follows:

(1) Husband–wife
(2) Father–children
(3) Father-in-law–daughter-in-law
(4) Siblings

While studying the pattern of interaction in all the four pairs of relationships, we shall be guided by the traditionally prescribed interaction pattern and will try to evaluate how far the pattern revealed is in conformity with the normative postulations. Here we will also analyse the differences in the interaction pattern of the nuclear and the joint families as operating in all the four pairs of relationships under review while discussing different aspects related with the internal processes of the family. For example, in the chapter on division of labour and power and authority we have discussed several aspects of the widespread social inequality between men and women. We have also observed there the significant role played by age, sex and relationships' roles in governing internal processes in the family. By implication the discussion of all these aspects involved questions of interaction pattern among different members of the family. But all these were done earlier in a very general way. Here we have probed deep into the phenomenon by isolating and specifying different pairs of relationship. However, here we have focused our attention on the norms governing day-to-day interaction of the members.

Finally, in the last part of this chapter we have tried to study the mutual aid pattern between a nuclear family of parents with geographically separated family of his son/sons or the nuclear family of a son with the geographically separated family of his/their parents. This will reveal the extent to which geographical separation weakens kinship ties.

Husband-Wife Relationship

A society based on the demands of a rigid form of community implies considerable sacrifice on the part of its members, both male and female. There is little privacy for any one. Rules of conduct and duties are strictly enjoined. Traditional Hindu opinion discouraged the intense overt interaction between husband and wife. A woman is revered as mother, not as wife. Overt expression of intimacy and emotion might cause friction in regard to other family relationships. In order to describe the pattern of husband-wife relationship, we quote a passage with regard to traditional Japan. In a way this portrays the pattern traditionally prevailing in Hindu India also.

> "In their role as bearers and rearers of children women were necessary mechanical appurtenances to a scheme of social structure which has provisions for continuity that involved many people and

which was made to see far more important than the relations between any two individuals. Proper men did not admit to romantic love for their wives, instead they spoke of them as lowly creatures (Horbeck, 1965 : 13).

Likewise, the values of the Hindu joint family denigrate conjugal relationship. The values aimed at limiting the significance of the husband-wife intimacy (Gore, 1968). "In a joint family, the daughter-in-law does not have any independence unless she becomes the mother of two or three children. Efforts at endearment, smiling or even exchange of glances would be enough to cause comment and would earn for the couple a reputation for being a shameless" (Dube, 1955 : 145). In fact, the husband and wife did not go out for walks or social visits and the practice is yet not common (Goode, 1968).

Against this background now we proceed to analyse the pattern of relationships between husband and wife in different types of families. Here, the pattern of segregation in social life between husband and wife has been studied in the area of social visitings and even with regard to going to the pictures. In order to observe the extent of closeness in conjugal relationship, we asked respondent to say if the couples of their families visit certain places together. The responses tabulated in Table 4.1 show that the norms prescribed by tradition prohibiting husband and wife going together is still strictly adhered to in many cases.

Table 4.1 : Family type and percentages of couples going out together to different places

Place of visit	*Young Couple*		*Old Couple*	
	Nuclear	*Joint*	*Nuclear*	*Joint*
No where	16.4	17.5	12.5	26.5
Market	68.8	65.0	71.7	60.7
Cinema	73.9	77.5	37.5	25.0
Dinner	54.7	40.0	45.6	46.4
Public meetings	13.0	12.5	12.5	5.0
Libraries	12.3	7.5	5.1	7.1
Hotels	39.7	37.5	12.5	3.5
Clubs	0.0	0.0	2.5	0.0

In both the types of family a majority of couples does not go out together to any of the seven places mentioned in the schedule, "going out together is a small index of equaliterianism" (Goode, *ibid*), yet this appears to be a total stranger in good number of families. In joint family this can be explained by the fact that married life starts under the presence of a number of elder relatives and, in the years immediately after marriage, any overt expression of concern for each other by couples is unwarranted. In fact, no importance is attached to the personal life of the young couple. As a newly-married youngman from a joint family narrated:

> "I have been married only two months back. Even now I cannot meet my wife in day time. In the day time she is always surrounded by mother, sisters and younger brother. I always wish to go with my wife to many places. As she has never come to Patna before, I can show her a number of interesting places. But, I know, I can never do so at present; for even if I wish to take her to cinema, my sisters would go along with us."

In another Joint Family Father-in-law tells

> "In my life there is strict adherence to joint family norms. In order to keep under control conjugal intimacy, I have made an arrangement. Whenever any daughter-in-law of mine feels like to going to any place she will take any one of her husband's younger brothers. In this way I have given the freedom necessary for her and yet the intimacy of the conjugal bonds remains under control."

In case of the nuclear families, absence of the practice of going out together to these places may well be attributed to the traditional type of orientation of such couples or their extremely busy household life. As a respondent from a nuclear family told:

> "I am a businessman and I get little time to devote to family activities. My wife often complaints that we do not go together even to see movies. I can do nothing but to feel sorry."

Another respondent again from a nuclear family mentions care of children as the main factor inhibiting him going out with his wife. To quote the respondent:

"After my marriage, my father-in-law also came to my residence and stayed. Consequently so long as he remained with us, I never went with my wife to any place. He left us after a year and by that time I was father of a child. Now I have three small children. It is very difficult to go somewhere with children and at the same time quite impossible to leave them alone in the home."

However, the percentage of families where the practice of going out together by couples is permitted is greater as compared to those families where these things are prohibited. In fact, one of the most visible trends of the changing family has been the growth of and encouragement to intimate attachment between spouses. A wife today is expected to be companion, confidante to her husband. Consequently it is expected that she would enjoy life and not be neglected. Table (4.1) shows that cinema, market and places of community dinner are mostly visited by young couples. Visits to hotels occupy the next position and visit to libraries and places of public meeting are of least concern to the young couples. In the case of the older couples market is the only place visited by majority of couples. Visits to cinemas and places of community dinner come next. Libraries, public meetings, hotels, clubs are the places attracting only a few couples. This comparison points out that the places of recreation are visited only by young couples, while the older couples go out together mostly for shopping. Then, the, majority of the young couples appears to visit more than one of the places mentioned in the schedule. This, however, does not appear to be the position with the older couples. This comparison can be used as an index of change because it highlights the fact that the contemporary social definitions put a high premium upon the conjugal relationship than in the past. In fact, this corroborates the postulation that "the quality of inter-personal relations between husband and wife changes as they leave one stage of life and enter another" (Dube, *op. cit.,* 142).

If we relate the family type with the extent of going out together by couples of different generations we find that in the case of the younger generations, family type does not make any difference so far as rigidity in observance of traditional norms of not going together by couples is concerned. But in the case of the couples of older generation we find that in the observance of these norms, difference in family composition does make a spot. We find that these norms have the curious habit of intensifying themselves in joint family. Conventions of former times are being discouraged by romantic individualism of the younger generation irrespective of their family composition. In this respect the changes induced by industrialism and urbanization evoke identical reaction from all types of family. But in the case of older generation either due to their traditional orientation or due to their eagerness for system maintenance, the couples of joint families are more rigid than the respondents of nuclear families. Barring only few exceptions among all types of couples we find that in-so-far as percentages of couples visiting different places are concerned, nuclear family couples appear to be more egalitarian than joint family couples[1]. This is not surprising. To live as a small family in an urban area means a profound change for both husband and wife. With the establishment of a nuclear household the nature and tone of husband-wife relationship undergoes a significant modification. Now they are free to run their own affairs. This is not the position in joint family where the relationship of husband and wife is not very crucial. The joint family contains persons who are at par in age and sex for different types of members and both the spouses can do without each other so far as entertainment and recreation are concerned.

For the sake of system maintenance and to prohibit overt expression of intimacy between husband and wife, traditional prohibits free mixing inside the house where a number of relatives are present. Particularly in joint family, the presence of a number of relatives limits their freedom to mix with each other. Out of fear and respect of elder relatives and due to the fear of setting a wrong precedent, couples restrain themselves from mixing freely with each other even in the house itself. In order to see to what extent and in what way new role of definition of the family has affected the limitations impounded on free mixing of couples, we inquired from joint family respondents whether in their families a couple talks to each other in the presence of others. The tabulation of responses shows that only in case of 28.3 per cent of joint families, spouses do not talk freely with each other. In the case of a number of families, tradition seems to be the dominant factor governing interaction pattern between husband and wife. To talk freely with one's life-partner in the presence of other relatives is also a small index of equalitarianism, yet we find that this is also not allowed in a number of families. Modern conditions of life providing increasing encouragement to romantic love between spouses are not strong enough to counter the strongholds of tradition in these cases. We cite here a peculiar case which depicts one unfavourable reaction against the intimacy between spouses. This is from a joint family:

"When my brother was married, he was the eldest married male in the family. Since both the husband and wife were highly educated my family witnessed many new things. For the first time my mother saw that a wife can dine with her husband. In fact she was greatly disturbed. And she talked about this incident to a number of relatives. But she could not talk about all this to my very serious elder brother. Ultimately my mother reconciled herself but could not suppress her anger for her first daughter-in-law."

Father-Child Relationship

The traditional pattern of father-child relationship tends to be characterised by respect and obedience. The father is a symbol of authority and the child is required to respect and fear him. The relationship is characterised by formalised deference customs depicting fear, respect and inequality of real power. There is a cultural expectation of submissiveness on the part of the child. In order to see to what extent father is perceived as a symbol of terror and fear, we asked a question as to why he is respected in the family? That is, to say, to what extent a father receives respect from his child only on account of his terror and dominance? The data, however, show that with the advent of urbanization there is greater equality in father-child relationship. Only a minority of children (above five years of age) respect their father out of fear and terror in 26.8 per cent of the cases in nuclear families while the figure is of the tune of 29.9 per cent in the case of joint families. Instead of terror and fear, the father-offspring relationship seems to be guided more by emotion and understanding. Due to the existence of a larger number of aged, married and self-dependent offsprings in case of the joint family, as against the nuclear family, there appears to be greater prevalence of love and affection as the factor guiding the father-child relationship in joint family than nuclear family.

Father-in-law–Daughter-in-law Relationship

The expected pattern of interaction between a father-in-law and his daughter-in-law is that of avoidance. In fact only in exceptional circumstances one may come into contact with another. It is believed that relationship of avoidance between the father-in-law and his daughter-in-law contributes considerably towards the maintenance of the family system. In fact, development of any liberal emotional relation "would have threatened the accepted political solutions of the kinship structure and the entire position of the mother-in-law on which the household organization depended" (Levy; 1949:185). Now, the typical tradition-observing family is usually the joint family than the nuclear family. In order to see this we found out the extent to which father-in-law and his daughter-in-law maintain relation of avoidance in such families. The data as contained in Table 4.2 shows that the joint family conforms more than the nuclear family to this norm.

Table 4.2 : Extent of avoidance between the Father-in-law and Daughter-in-law Relationship by family type

Type of the Family	*Extent of avoidance*		
	Complete avoidance %	*Little avoidance** %	*No avoidance* %
Nuclear	14.2	57.1	28.6
Joint	42.9	37.1	20.1

* Little avoidance means contacting each other only in time of great necessity.

Table 4.2 reveals that the majority of nuclear families is less inclined to attach importance to the avoidance relation than joint family. In nuclear family, the families completely ignore any relationship. This only shows that nuclear family is more and more shifting towards new patterns of family inter action than joint family. In nuclear family the contact with one another is made more necessary as well as frequent because of the absence of wide range of relationship

One of our respondents from a nuclear family observed:

> "Prior to the death of my wife, I do not remember any instance when I came into contact with my daughter-in-law. But after her death I have to be dependent on her for a lot of things. Even if I have to take food I would have to contact her. If there is any trouble to her children and her husband is away on his job, she will have to call me."

Sibling Relationship

In the Hindu family the relationship between siblings is of great importance, sometimes, even for the continuance of the unit. Karve (1953) says good brotherliness is an ideal for the joint family. So far as the relationship between brother and sister is concerned it is quite significant for joint family. "While the brother-brother relationship may be very close, it rarely approaches the tenderness and affection of brother-sister relationship" (Gore, *op. cit.,* p.11). Changes in the sister-sister relationship are "perhaps the least likely to cause disruption and strain to the family structure" (Ross, 1961 : 166), yet the relationship between sisters during early childhood is likely to affect their socialization in late life when they become daughters-in-law. The emotion of jealousy internalized during early childhood may greatly affect her adjustment with any other sister-in-law in the family of in-laws.

However, spelling out the cardinal principle governing sibling relationship in the Hindu family, we can say that age takes precedence. Younger siblings have to obey and respect their elders. The position of siblings as between themselves is very much a matter of their age sequences. Table 4.3 contains pattern of inter-relationship between siblings above fifteen years of age. Table 4.3 shows that in majority of families, both nuclear and joint, the sibling relationship is characterised by the growth of friendly affection in only a few cases.

Table 4.3 : Family type and the pattern of sibling relationship

Family Type	*Type of Relationship**			
	Fear and respect %	*Respect* %	*Friendly* %	*Neglect* %
Nuclear	78.2	10.9	7.3	3.6
Joint	65.0	17.5	15.0	2.5

* Pattern of relationship, here, refers to pattern of relationship maintained by a younger sibling for an elder sibling.

However, if we examine the role of family type as a variable in governing sibling relationship we find that the elder siblings of the nuclear families are respected with or without fear in a slightly increased number of instances than those of the joint families.

In making sibling relationship, a relationship of friendship, the joint family appears to be ahead of the nuclear family. This may partly be explained by the fact that in the joint families there is greater likelihood of the existence of aged or old siblings with each having his own children and economic independence of brothers. It is apparent from Table 4.3 that the nuclearization of family alone does not necessarily leads to democratization of relationship among siblings. Below we cite two cases to show that fear and respect may not be principles governing sibling relationship in joint families.

> "When my younger brother was unmarried he feared as well as respected me. But after his marriage there have been clashes between myself and him, on a number of occasions. Since my widow-mother doesn't like that we should get separated during her life time, we are any how living together. As a result I seldom even talk to my brother and he also avoids me.

> "We the respondent and his brother are now above forty years of age. Each brother has a lot of responsibilities. We have sons and daughters who fear and respect both of us. Since my younger brother himself is middle-aged, I do not see why he should fear and respect me. In fact, I have given him complete freedom in family affairs. We discuss each and every problem like a friend. This I have conceded deliberately for my brother. Because this will save my joint family."

But before we close this discussion on sibling relationship, we want to admit that due to the nature of the design, we, unfortunately, could not take into account the age and sex differences of siblings in order to see their impact upon sibling relationships. Only a very general type of picture, touching only the surface of the phenomenon, is available here.

Geographical Isolation and Interactional Propinquity

It is conventional to view urban life as characterised by a decrease in the kinship view. Because "as contacts tend to be more intimate and controls more effective when relatives live geographically close, so separation of the members and household units will tend to have opposite effect" (Ross, *op. cit.,* 33). Therefore, I propose to analyse the nature of relation between a parents' nuclear family with their sons' family or a son's nuclear family with his parents' family when the two are living separately at different places. This would reveal how far geographical separation affects inter-generational link and, secondly, to what extent the nuclear family is isolated from the family of traditionally most close relatives (parents or sons). In other words, we will try to examine to what extent the relationship between a nuclear family of son or parents and the family of his parents or their son, living in different households depicts the supposed characteristics of the extended kin network. The relationship between two such households has been analysed in terms of the mutual aid patterns between such families. From the analysis of Table 4.4 it appears that even though parents' families and sons' families live apart geographically, in a majority of cases they help each other in time of need. Help at the time of sickness appears to be the most important area of mutual assistance among all the items contained in the schedule. In fact, Hindu norms put a heavy premium on help to be rendered on such occasions. "A son failing in duty of providing adequately for his old parents and not caring sufficiently for their comforts, particularly during illness, invites strong social disapproval and comment. He is regarded as a bad example" (Dube, *op. cit.*, 152). The parents too have a stronger affectionate bonds with their children. "When the husband gazes at the children of his wife as though he were looking at his own image in a mirror, he experiences the same joy as does the pure man who has been given his place in his heaven" (Bachmann, 1942: 151). In the same way mother was expected to have utmost attachment for her children. It is but natural for parents, also, to help their son at least when some one is ill in his family. Here we cite one example of a son having practically no connection with his parents but feeling it his duty to help them at the time of their illness.

> "I live away from my parents' family. My father also earns. But we have seldom helped each other financially, my mother does not even like to live with my family. But when few years back I came to know that she had been seriously injured and was confined to bed I could not do anything else than to help and nurse her. In fact, my wife, who cannot happily live with my mother even for a day, persuaded me to go to bring her to our residence, because this was our duty."

Noted below is the case of a son regarding the help he has received from his parents.

"After giving birth to two children my wife does not keep good health. She frequently falls ill. Children are small and I have to neglect them in order to earn money. But since my parents are alive I am slightly less worried about my wife and children. Even if a post card is dropped they will immediately rush out to help. I do not know what shape future will take, but this much is certain that if my parents are not alive, I might not get this type of assistance from my brothers."

Table 4.4: Mutual aid-pattern between geographically separated nuclear families of parents and children

Items of Mutual Aid	*Percentage of persons receiving*	*Percentage of persons not receiving*
1. Help from son to parents at the time of sickness in family	85.3	14.7
2. Help in the shape of advice on money matter by son to parents	70.0	30.0
3. Help from parents to son's family at the time of sickness in family	92.3	7.7
4. Help in the shape of advise on money matter by parents to son	70.3	29.7
5. Son making sacrifice for his parents	78.4	21.6

Table 4.4 shows that in the case of helping in money or business matters, parents and sons are not so communicative with each other than helping at the time of sickness. It is evident that in money or business matters individualistic trends are prevailing. The economic factor accentuates the isolation between the two families. However, in a good number of cases the sons are even prepared to make any sacrifice for their parents. In other words, when occasion demands, it at least appears that the nuclear families of the sons will give up every thing to help their parents. Table 4.4 further reveals that the parents are more likely to provide succour than their sons especially at the time of illness. If this is an indicator of any trend, then it can be said that old persons are more inclined towards maintaining tradition than the younger ones.

Closing this chapter, we can say that in this chapter the focus of study has been the changing interactional pattern in the family. We have endeavoured to explore the pattern of interaction between certain pairs of relationships. To find out the trend of change in the interactional pattern we have compared the pattern revealed in different types of families with the traditionally prescribed interaction pattern. We found that going out together with one's wife, which is a small index of equalitarianism, is still not prevalent in a number of families, both nuclear and joint. In fact, the norm prohibiting one to go out with his wife is not a social fiction. However, in a majority of the families of both the types the tradition in this connection has been broken. It is also found that places of recreation are visited more by young couples than the older couples. Thus, we found that the tone of husband-wife relationship changes with change in the stages of life. Family type, as a variable, is not important in the case of young couples in-so-far as observance of traditional norm of not going together by couples is concerned. We, however, found that in the case of old couples those norms have a curious habit of intensifying themselves in the joint family. Then to talk freely with one's wife is also a very small index of equalitarianism, yet we found that even this is not allowed in a number of joint families.

In fact, modern conditions of life have failed to weaken the strongholds of tradition in many cases. We further found that there is greater equality in father-child relationship today. In the case of joint family, however, there appears to be greater prevalence of love and affection as the factor guiding the father-child relationship. The joint family was much more conformist than the nuclear family to tradition prescribing relation of avoidance between a father-in-law and his daughter-in-law. In the matter of sibling relationship, the joint family comprising aged or economically independent siblings demonstrates greater equalitarianism than the nuclear family. In the last part of this chapter, we have analysed mutual aid pattern of a nuclear family with the geographically separated family of parents or son. We have found that geographical isolation does not dampen the mutual aid pattern of such families.

NOTE

1. It must be noted here that in some cases the difference is small and in others it is very marked.

5

THE STRUCTURE OF POWER AND AUTHORITY IN THE FAMILY

THE ANALYSIS of the power-structure of the family is considered to be a central theme in many theoretical and empirical analyses of the family. In fact, there are "cogent theoretical grounds and even some empirical evidences which indicate that a knowledge of the support and power structure of the family is essential for an understanding of almost all aspects of family functioning including, for example, familial effectiveness, in socialization and control of behaviour, and in maintaining the allegiance of the members to the family group". (Straus and Cetrynbaum, 1963: 138). For the smooth and proper functioning of families it is but necessary that there should be a clear cut pattern of power distribution. There must be a web consisting of centres of authority to regulate and co-ordinate familial activities. All normal families have a certain power structure and authority pattern. That is to say, there exists some pattern of internal differentiation based on power and status. So far as the traditional Hindu family is concerned the authority was generally exercised by the eldest male of the family. (Gore, 1968:135) points out that the system maintenance of the joint family requires a clear cut pattern of authority which is "met by the norm that the authority is vested in the eldest male member of the family". "Since most decisions were based upon tradition.....age was as effective a basis for authority as any other" (Goode, 1968:247). In brief these postulations highlight two important characteristics of power-structure in the traditional Hindu family, *viz.*, (i) prevalence of centralised pattern of authority instead of diffused, and (ii) norm of making the eldest man as the centre of corporate authority.

In this chapter, therefore, we propose (i) to discern the way in which power is distributed among the members of the families; and (ii) to find out how far the patterns revealed are congruent with the normative extrapolations. But before we proceed with these objectives, let us first define power and delineate the process of the exercise of power by individual members of the family. We define power as an act or statement which indicates an attempt on the part of a family member to control, initiate, change or modify the behaviour or motivation of another member of the same family. Now, since a decision is a policy likely to control, initiate, change or modify the behaviour of others, an assessment of locus of power can be made to a considerable extent by analysing the pattern of involvement in the decision-making process of family. Dahl (1963), Mills (1963), Laswell and Kaplan (1950), Hill (1965) all consider involvement in decision-making to be an important method for the study of power structure. While, according to Dahl (*op. cit.*, 52), this method "pierces the facade of formal position and reputation by studying participation in decisions", Mills (*op. cit.*) stresses that the problem of who is involved in making these is the basic problem of power, to Laswell and Kaplan (*op. cit.*) power itself consists in the participation in the making of decision and to Hill (*op. cit.*) decision-making pattern forms one of the two relevant expressions of family role structure so far as identification of locus of power in the family is concerned.

For the purpose of the present study we have tried to obtain an appraisal of the locus and structure of power in the family by analysing the pattern of decision-making. To elaborate the procedure, we have asked the respondents to name those members of their families whom they perceive as taking decisions with regard to certain issues. Next, we have also asked the respondents to name these members in order of their effectiveness so far as making of decisions is concerned. Lastly, for those families among whom there has not been any occasion for making decisions with regard to any of these items, we have asked the respondents as to who would be the person involved in decision-making if such occasion arises. For such families also centres of authority are to be mentioned in order of their effectiveness in decision-making. The issues with which the power-wielding pattern has been studied are as follows:

(a) Schooling of children
(b) Choice of bride
(c) Choice of bridegroom
(d) Giving permission to wife or daughter-in-law to meet her parents
(e) Bringing in relatives

Even after taking these precautions, there might be certain limitations to this method of locating power in families (particularly on the basis of perception of respondents) but such limitations are not exclusive in this area alone. In fact, as Dahl (*op. cit.*, 53) puts "None is fool-proof". We now proceed to analyse the structure and exercise of power in different types of family.

Tables 5.1 (a), (b) reveal the most effective centres of authority as apparent from the perception of individual respondents. Now if we examine the role of the eldest man as the most powerful centre of authority, we find that with regard to all the five issues the eldest man is perceived as the most effective centre in the power structure of family. In the case of nuclear family, however, this might not be an indicative of authority established by eldest man only by seniority in age. In the nuclear family, the eldest man happens to be, in most of the cases, the only adult male in family. In such cases he might be the centre of most effective authority. However, so far as the joint family is concerned we find a pattern of power wielding which appears to be quite discrepant from the normative patterns. This will be quite apparent if we examine the extent to which eldest man assumes the role of the most powerful leader. So far as the joint family is concerned on all the five issues the eldest man appears to be wielding less power than those of the nuclear families. It appears that the traditional base of power (based on seniority of age) available to the eldest man is not so powerful. Members of the joint family appear to pull themselves away from exercise of power by the eldest man. For a detailed analysis, we now examine the authority role of different categories of persons issue-wise in the two types of the family.

First, in taking a decision on schooling the eldest man appears to be the most effective point in the power structure of both types of families. But in the joint family, individual heads of different sub-units seem to be the final authority in a good number of cases. This is indicative of the weakening of the corporate authority of the joint family as symbolised in the eldest man. However, this weakening of corporate authority, even to this extent, is restricted to the sphere of education and can be explained by the fact that in these days education has become a key factor in determining the future social and economic status of a man. It is, therefore, but natural for the individual parents to see that right decisions are taken with regard to schooling of their children.

Table 5.1(a): Family type and perception of final authority by respondents

Areas of decision-making	*Final decision-makers (percentage)*									
	Eldest man		*Eldest Woman*		*Child's father**		*Child's mother***		*Others*	
	Nuclear	*Joint*	*Nuclear*	*Joint*	*Nuclear*	*Joint*	*Nuclear*	*Joint*	*Nuclear*	*Joint*
1. Schooling	89.0	64.3	2.8	0	1.8	28.6	0.9	0.0	5.5	7.1
2. Selection of bride	60.4	47.5	15.8	35.0	2.0	10.0	0.0	0.0	11.9	7.5
3. Selection of bridegroom	74.5	65.7	10.8	20.0	2.8	5.7	0.0	0.0	11.8	3.6
4. Permission of women going home to their parents	80.0	50.0	18.0	29.5	0.9	2.3	0.0	4.5	0.9	13.6

* In the case of the issue concerning permission for women going home to their parents, father-in-law of the women concerned.

** In the case of the issue concerning permission for women going home to their parents, mother-in-law of the women concerned.

Table 5.1(b): Family type and perception of final authority by respondents

Area of decision-making	*Final decision-makers (percentage)*					
	Eldest Man		*Eldest Woman*		*Others*	
	Nuclear	*Joint*	*Nuclear*	*Joint*	*Nuclear*	*Joint*
Bringing in relatives	81.6	71.8	7.7	17.9	10.7	10.2

This is particularly the case where the father of the child is more educated than the eldest man. A Harijan respondent gave the following experience:

> "Fortunately my son is a good student and in a year or two he would become a doctor. For his education, I have provided the necessary finance by making shoes. As a student, he has always taken necessary decisions with regard to his education himself. Naturally if his children are to be educated, I cannot be expected to take necessary decisions."

But similar situation may arise even in the case of families where the father of the child and the eldest male are equally educated. As the head of a joint family narrated:

> "As my grand-daughter grew up, my son decided to send her to a school. I did not like this decision. My daughter-in-law is educated enough to teach a child like my grand-daughter. In our own days we believed in giving girls education only upto primary stage and that too even in home. Even today my belief is this that girls should not be allowed to get education in a school, rather arrangements for private tuition should be made. But my son did not agree with my attitudes and ultimately his decision prevailed."

Now, so far as the decision with regard to selection of bridegrooms and brides are concerned, we witness a further decline in the authority of the eldest man. We also find that in the selection of a bride for a family member, after the eldest man, eldest woman is perceived to be the next important centre of authority. This exercise of power by eldest woman would signify a modernizing and liberalizing tendency in the power structure of the nuclear family, but for the joint family this would stand for something else also. In the case of the joint family it highlights the fact that where the eldest man becomes weak as the most effective centre in decision-making, the power thus relinquished does not necessarily lead to the growth of individualistic pattern of decision-making, rather shift of authority from eldest man to his wife goes to solidify a pattern of authority which is at least not inimical to the maintenance of the joint family system. The decline in the symbolic authority of the traditional centre of authority gets compensated by a shift of authority to the eldest woman. The latter can dominate the younger members of the family through affection and love.

The head of a joint family observed:

> "When we were growing up, my father was very strict. We were often punished by him even for minor mistakes. When we were grown up in spite of the fact that the strictness of my father did not matter for us, yet out of fear we seldom talked to our father. As a result if I had to get certain things done according to my own wishes, I used to convince my all-affectionate mother and being herself dominant she used to get the things decided according to her own wishes and my father never objected."

Another respondent again from a joint family said:

> "I am the *de facto* head of a joint family. My entire family is under my control. I have a widow-mother, who never objects to my decisions. However, when the question of my own marriage came, I left to her the authority to negotiate. This I did deliberately because I know that if I arrange my marriage by myself my mother would be most unhappy."

Another member of a joint family spelt out reasons for the supreme authority of the eldest woman (in this case the wide-mother) as follows:

> "I never had a good relation with my elder brother who is more interested in his own welfare than the welfare of the family. As a result, in all matters my mother is the final authority to decide, because we two brothers cannot doubt her impartiality."

Roughly, similar pattern of power-wielding appears to exist in the case of decision concerning the selection of bridegroom, with the only difference that the percentage of persons perceiving the eldest man as the final decision-maker increases. This increase, however, might be attributed to the system of marriage itself, where for the selection of a bridegroom such troubles persist which can only be tackled by elder men. The scope of choice being not so wide.

Then, so far as the issue concerning permission to a relative to live with the family is concerned, once again we find that in most of the families final authority lies with the eldest man in both types of the families. Next to him, in the exercise of power comes the position of the wife of the eldest man. This is in conformity with the pattern noticed in the case of two issues above. The decline in the percentage of persons perceiving eldest male as the most effective centre of power is not so high as is the position in the case of decision on schooling and selection of bride. But in the case of decision on permission for women going to their parents, the eldest man is perceived as the most effective centre in decision-making in lesser number of cases than the previous one, once again raising the power-wielding capacity of the eldest woman.

On the pattern of wielding power as depicted in the ability to be perceived as the most influential centre in decision-making, we can point out, first, that the respondents' perception of eldest man's role as final authority in decision-making varies in different regions of decision-making. And even where eldest man is there at the top of the family hierarchy, in practice, his traditional role as the most dominant centre of familial power appears to be absent. The stratum wherein the eldest man is perceived as the most effective centre of decision-making is the nuclear family. This, however, can be explained by the possibility of his being the only adult man to take responsible decisions. But in the joint families, the families where the eldest man is perceived as the most effective centre of authority are in lesser percentage than in the nuclear families. In the second place, on the whole, after the oldest man the oldest woman is perceived to be the next influential centre in family decision-making in the both types of the family in all cases except schooling. However, the presence of individualistic pattern of decision-making only in the case of schooling cannot be regarded as any threat to the corporate authority of eldest man of the joint family. It merely hints at the anxiety of the individuals with regard to the proper schooling of their children. Next, we also find that in all the issue-areas women appear to be low powered in relation to men so far as wielding of power is concerned. Perhaps, the notion that men should be dominant is too deeply ingrained to respond radically to an outside stimulus. Lastly, the decision of schooling, bringing in relatives and permission for women going home to their parents are the areas where decision-making pattern is more in conformity with verbalised norms than the other cases. This is the position in the case of the nuclear family. In case of the joint family this extent of conformity with traditional norms is visible in none of the areas. However, admission of relatives, selection of bridegroom and schooling are the areas where conformity with verbalised norms is greater as compared to other areas.

After discerning the extent to which the norm of vesting eldest man of the family with final authority is prevalent, we now proceed to analyse the pattern of decision-making as reflected by the number of persons participating in the decision-making process. The responses in Table 5.2 show that power structure of both groups of families is of centralised pattern in the majority of cases. Autocratic pattern of decision-making seems to be the characteristic of all the five behavioural areas selected for study. In other words, the traditional outlook of having centralised pattern of power structure is quite strong in the Hindu family. However, the Table 5.2 further shows that the autocratic pattern of decision-making is more a characteristic of joint family than the nuclear family. The larger percentage of shared decision-making in case of the nuclear family corresponds to tendency of the nuclear family members to shift their role conception in an egalitarian direction more readily than the joint family. In case of the nuclear family, the decision on mate selection appears to be more egalitarian than others. On the other hand, in case of the joint family, mate selection and schooling appear to be more egalitarian areas than others.

To sum up, in this chapter, on the basis of certain relevant literature we have found that traditional Hindu family is characterised by the prevalence of centralised pattern of authority and norm of making eldest man as the locus of corporate authority. Then we tried find out how far the patterns revealed are in conformity with normative postulation. We find that eldest man remains the final and most effective centre of authority in a majority of families. The stratum in which eldest man is perceived as the most effective centre in decision-making by largest number of respondents is the nuclear family. This, however, is explained by the fact that in nuclear families he is the only adult male to take responsible decisions. Secondly, women appear to be low powered in comparison in all the issue-areas. In joint families, the authority of eldest man has shifted to considerable degree to the eldest woman and in case of decision on schooling, the most striking feature is individualistic pattern of decision-making. This has been attributed to the anxiety of individual parents with regard to schooling of their children. The study has also revealed that autocratic pattern of decision-making instead of being syncratic is quite strong in Hindu family. However, the autocratic pattern of decision-making appeared to be more strong in joint family than nuclear family.

Table 5.2: Pattern of Decision-making by Family Type

(Figures in percentage)

Areas of decision making	*Prevalence of autocratic decision-making pattern*		*Prevalence of syncratic decision-making pattern*	
	Nuclear	*Joint*	*Nuclear*	*Joint*
1. Schooling	75.4	71.7	24.6	28.3
2. Selection of bride	50.9	71.7	49.0	28.3
3. Selection of bridegroom	51.8	63.0	48.0	37.0
4. Permission of women going home to their parents	64.9	76.10	35.0	24.0
5. Bringing in relatives	65.8	82.6	34.2	17.4

6

WORK AND THE FAMILY

THE RECENT economic history of India is heralded by a change from agriculture to industry as basis of economic life. With the advent of Britishers "the economic set-up of villages forced the peasants to leave their homes and go to towns to seek employment in more lucrative posts created by Westernized administrative machinery" (Chhibar, 1968:44). The last three centuries have witnessed far-reaching increase in job opportunity resulting in change in occupation by large numbers of Indians (Pandit, 1965). It is said that changes in occupational structure in India led to the weakening of joint family system. In order to get a new job a man is often required to leave his native place and settle in some other place. This implies a change in the composition of his residential family from joint to nuclear. Living jointly at one place becomes impossible by conditions of urban living, and at times leaving one's family becomes impossible by conditions of urban living, and at times leaving one's family becomes a necessity for him. The attitudes of family members towards occupations carrying diverse social sanctions may affect the choice of occupation by an individual of that family. In the third place, economic potentialities of the families of different types are also likely to reduce or enhance the toil, torture and bitterness faced by or accorded to an educated unemployed which in turn will affect inter-personal relationship in the family. Kinship structure and occupational pattern seem to be related with each other in more than one way.

The present chapter, therefore, is an attempt to study the inter-relation of the economic and familial structure. We will analyse the problem of educated unemployment (only male) and the strains felt by each person in different types of families,. the attitudes of respondents of different types with regard to role of education as means to achieve employment, changing prestige of occupations and occupational careers of women.

Problem of Educated Unemployed

"The growth of modern education in India was not paralleled by a proportional economic development of the country. As a result of this disparity, unemployment among the educated class had already assumed serious proportions by the end of the nineteenth century" (Desai, 1948:183). In fact, unemployment in the educated classes of today is not a new phenomenon in India, "it is conceivable that present conditions now cause it to be felt more heavily by a greater number of Hindus" (Ross, 1961:192). Unemployment places great strain on the family. The despair of an educated unemployed and the impatience of his guardians may lead to strained relationships in family. If we analyse the attitudes of families towards their educated unemployment males we find that joint family members show greater patience towards unemployed educated of their families than the members in nuclear families (Table 6.1). As in joint families there is a likelihood that there will be more than one earning member, it is better equipped to help unemployed persons than the nuclear family. It is considered to be a security and is bound to show stronger solidarity in times of crisis and need. Hence if educated unemployed are burden for lesser number of joint families than nuclear families, it is not surprising.

Table 6.1 : Attitudes of the families of different types towards educated educated unemployed males

Types of reaction towards educated unemployed male	Family type: Nuclear %	Family type: Joint %
1. He should take up any job, because he is a burden on the family	64.3	54.5
2. He should have patience and should not join a lowly occupation	14.3	18.2
3. The family thinks nothing for such persons	21.4	27.3

An unemployed youngman from a joint family observed:

> "I have passed B.A., but till now I could not get a job. My parents are old and traditional. Without considering that I am unemployed, they arranged my marriage. At present my wife also lives with me

> and I feel at times disturbed and ashamed on account of the fact that even when I have responsibilities of my own, I am contributing nothing to my family's income. Yet while I am continuing my efforts to get a job, I am at least getting all types of financial help from the other earning members of my joint family."

Another respondent says:

> "I was a labour officer in a factory. But accidentally I lost my job. At that time, I was married and a child had been born to us. I remained unemployed for about one year. Had the other earning members of my joint family not rendered any help to me, I would have been in a miserable condition."

However, here, it should be noted that even in the nuclear family if income is quite sufficient and liabilities are not too many the parents or guardians may not consider educated unemployed as a 'burden' for the family, but a nuclear family with one earning member, whose income is not too much, cannot show much patience to wait indefinitely in search of a 'suitable' job. To make it quite clear we quote an informant from one of the nuclear families:

> "My elder brother was unemployed for nearly a year. As he passed diploma in textile engineering, my father sent him to Bombay for getting training in a textile mill. I know this would not have been possible if my father had been a low paid employee. Since he earns nearly one thousand a month, he could afford this. But I know a friend of my brother with the same educational qualification. Since his poor father cannot afford to send him somewhere for training, he is still unemployed."

The frustration of another educated unemployed is noted below:

> "I came from a nuclear family. After completing the diploma in mechanical engineering I am in search of a job. Three years have passed since I passed my final examination but still I am unemployed. I find my father very disturbed because he is the only earning member and has to marry several daughters. Not only his expectation of my contribution to family purse remained unfulfilled, he has to support an educated unemployed. (myself) also. I

am always disturbed. What will happen to me? How will my sisters be married? All these worries disturb me very much. Father also rebukes me frequently even for slight mistakes."

Education vs. Employment

This acuteness of problem of unemployment among the educated has a particular significance for urban communities, because it consists principally of educated persons whether employed or unemployed. Since education is a passport for employment, continuous increase in the number of unemployed persons may well affect the choice with regard to different forms of education. In words of one respondent:

"There was a time when the engineers were in great demand. Today the engineers are worst sufferers. If they are not taken in the job for which they have been trained they cannot even get the job of a clerk. Therefore, though my son could have got an admission for an engineering course, I have forced him to join a Medical college to become a doctor."

Hard competition for jobs implies hard labour on the part of students also. Because until and unless they have a good degree, nothing can be done. Consequently if a father finds that after educating his child up to M.A. he is fit for the job of a humble clerk, the father might not educate his other sons much if they are not very bright.

An informant from a joint family observed:

"My eldest brother is an M.A. At present he is a clerk. My next brother failed twice before he was declared successful in Matriculation. After passing the High school, he intended to join college. But my father did not allow him. The only logic my father had for him was 'you are too weak to do good in college' and ultimately you will utmost get the job of a clerk. Then why do not you try just now for it? Why to waste the money."

In order to see to what extent education is a means to get a job we asked from our respondents a hypothetical question which is as follows:

"If your son or any member of your family is a brilliant student, and he is getting a job what should he do." The answers to the question were to be put under two categories and they were:

(1) Should continue his studies, or
(2) Join the job and stop the study.

The responses show that a big majority (69.3 %) of respondents feel that the student should be allowed to continue his education. Here it should be noted that in the hypothetical question respondent had to consider the case of a 'brilliant' student. In such cases, in fact, most families attempt to see that their sons get all types of education. They make all attempts to see that children do good so that they may compete with other students. However, a further analysis of responses with regard to the question reveals that joint family respondents favour employment to education than nuclear family respondents (see Table 6.2).

Table 6.2 : Family type and preference for education over employment

Opinion	*Family type (% of persons saying 'yes')*	
	Nuclear	*Joint*
1. In case there is a choice between employment and education of a brilliant student, he should continue education	70.2	45.7
2. In case there is a choice between employment and education of a brilliant student, he should take the job and give up education.	29.8	54.3

The Table 6.2 shows that in their mental orientation, when compared with nuclear family, joint family respondents are more prone to immediate gratification instead of deferred gratification. Since the capacity to postpone immediate gratification for higher gain at a later period is held to be an index of modernization, joint family seems to be less modern than the nuclear family. The lack of such capacity in joint family respondents may be explained by the presence of wider responsibilities and liabilities in joint family as compared to the nuclear family.

Changing Prestige of Occupations

Traditional Hindu society is characterised by inheritance of occupation. For the maintenance of social system the inheritance of occupation was "an obligation for both fathers and sons, since it served to maintain order in relatively static society" (Anderson and Ishwaran, 1961:94).

Later on, the economic forces changed the occupational pattern of the people. There was a scramble for jobs in towns. The cosmopolitanism of urban life brought out changes in value attached to particular occupations. As a result, all those professions enjoying degrading status became acceptable to those who were dead against them. Economic factors compelled an individual of high familial status to accept an occupation which was previously considered to be fit for low status families. In spite of all these, from Table 6.3 it appears that traditional attitudes to occupations, considered lowly, have now radically changed.

Table 6.3 : Family types and attitude towards manual labour or the job of peon

Statement	*Family Type (Percentage of persons saying 'yes')*	
	Nuclear	*Joint*
1. Manual labour and the job of peon is derogatory to their status	65.8	52.2
2. Manual labour and the job of peon is not derogatory under the present changed circumstances	34.2	47.8

A majority of respondents (61.9 %) feel that manual labour or job of a peon is below the dignity of their status. For respondents enjoying low status in the traditional sense this would mean that due to the internalization of Sanskritik values, they also feel it derogatory to do manual work or to accept the job of a peon. For the respondents of high social status judged by the traditional norms this highlights the fact that even with the growth urbanism, social pull to keep away from such lowly occupations is intense and mere economic pulls are not sufficient to alter the values attached to traditionally degraded occupations. When an individual deviates from the traditional normative prescriptions it is not without strains. Here we have one respondent saying:

> "My father is a clerk. When he took ill and remained confined for years, in order to provide for my family I joined as a peon in Government office. At first I was ashamed of joining this job. My younger brother who was a college student assured me that as soon he gets the job of a clerk, my continuation in the present post will not be required. But when I decided to be a hawker to sell newspapers, my entire family reacted very strongly against it. They said for a boy of a Kayastha family it is absolutely derogatory."

Another informant from one of the families said:

> "I am a Rajput by caste. My grand-father was an agriculturist. But due to the growth of Patna town, the government acquired our land. As a result my father became a peon. It is quite derogatory for us to say anywhere that he is a peon because it is not in conformity with our caste status."

The Table 6.3 further reveals that the family type is also a significant variable determining attitudes of respondents towards these low status occupations. It highlights the fact that joint family respondents are less conservative in this regard as compared to nuclear family respondents. This goes to point out the fact that with increased urbanization and costlier urban life, large joint families are being guided less and less by social considerations. Due to poor returns from traditional occupations on the one hand and existence of various potential earners and persons of diverse statuses, joint family respondents are less rigid in rejecting lowly occupations than nuclear family respondents.

Women as Money-Earners

Hindu women have all along been regarded as the guardians of hearth and the mothers of children. The ideal before them was to grow up as obedient daughters and sisters and die as wives and they were confined mostly within the four-wall of the house. But the factors of urbanization and modernization cannot leave the position of women untouched. In middle-class families, mostly women did not work for money, in the past, but now by taking up remunerative jobs they have raised their status. If we take the number of women holding remunerative jobs to indicate their social status we can find to what extent they are enjoying equal opportunities with men. In our sample there are 10 women working for money (eight in nuclear family and two in joint family). This small number is an index of the fact that traditional conservativeness inhibiting rightful place of women in matter of holding remunerative occupations has not gone. The number is so small that we cannot see the impact of the composition of family on the chances of women's career. However, the detailed analysis of these cases reveals that all of the women thus doing some work for money are only secondary bread winners. They are just helping man in earning for the family. Next, it also became clear that occupational careers of these women are not continuous. It is the normal expectation that a man will be at work or seeking work from the time he is either grown up or has left his education and will work till his retirement or death. This is not the case with women earners. They have started earning even as manual workers when they were old enough for their families and had given birth to several children or became widows. Three respondents told that their wives worked so long they were issueless. After the birth of children they were busy whole time in household duties.

To quote one instance:

> "My wife was a school teacher. I have sufficient income to look after my family. In order to keep herself engaged she joined a school as a teacher. But after giving birth to a child it became difficult for us to allow her to continue in the job. In my opinion, had she neglected the child, we would have been more guilty, on the other hand leaving her job did not affect us in any way."

Another respondent told:

> "My wife was a teacher. After the birth of my first child, a maid-servant was employed by us to look after the child. The school was also very near to my residence. Thus everything was being managed but when my second child was born it became impossible for us to leave them in the care of the maid-servant. The school also shifted to a distant place. The job was given up. Still I am not sorry because that was the only course open for us."

Lastly, taking up occupational career may give rise to various comments and problems for the family. One informant told:

> "We have a tea stall. My mother looks after that. Now she is doing this because there is none to look after and without it we will be economically handicapped. But it is quite painful for us. Because her continuance in the business is considered to be a bad thing. At the time of marriage of any one from our family it becomes all the more soul-slaying, because we have to hide this truth."

To sum up, we can say that in this chapter the inter-relations between familial structure and occupation have been studied by analysing the problem of unemployment of educated males, role of education as an avenue to employment, changing prestige of occupations and the occupational careers of women. These facts have been studied and pictures emerging in two types of families have been compared. We have found that joint family members show greater patience towards educated unemployed than the nuclear family. This might be due to the possibility of there being more than one earning male in the joint family. In their mental orientations, joint family respondents are more prone to immediate gratification and are more ready to stop their education for employment than nuclear family. The joint family appears to be more prone to accept low status jobs than the nuclear family. Thus, due to economic factors while in their mental orientations the joint families are more inclined to ignore social considerations than the nuclear family, when the question of unemployed comes they are more helpful than their counterparts in the nuclear families. Lastly, women appear to be only supplementing their husbands who are primary bread-earners for the family. Their occupational career does not appear to be continuous and strains are often involved when women go to work for money.

7

CHANGING PATTERNS OF MARRIAGE

ACCORDING to the traditional Hindu view, marriage is a sacrament. It is "in essence a ritual and a formality, of course, very important through which an individual has to go, to be able to start his or her life in *Grihasth-ashrama*, that is, the householder's life" (Prabhu, 1954:150). It is not a civil contract, it is both a religious and social duty for Hindu men and women and "no normal man or woman must die without receiving it" (Karve, 1953:130). This, being a *sanskar* of the Hindus, is conceived to impart purification to the individual concerned. This is an important ritual in a way necessary to him because perpetuation of the patriline is believed to be the sacred duty of every Hindu" without which his soul would not get its transmigration and reincarnation" (Goode, 1968). "These views regarding Hindu marriage have come down from the ancient Vedic times making Hindu parents believe that the marriage of their children is one of their most sacred duties (Ross, 1961). The traditional pattern of Hindu marriage, limitation of choice by exogamous and endogamous prohibitions, marriage by arrangement, lack of marital freedom, indissoluble nature of marriage, prohibition of widow marriage, etc., these facets of the traditional marriage system had a significantly contributing influence towards the maintenance of caste system and the joint family pattern, which, in turn, along with self-sufficient nature of the Indian village were responsible for "continuance of cultural traditions" in India (Kapadia, 1959).

Since the norms and mores surrounding marriage are usually deeply set, we, in this chapter, propose to study in what way the system of Hindu marriage is adjusting and changing. That is to say, the study is an attempt to examine the impact of modern trends represented by formal education, urbanization and ideological clashes on such traditions as are associated with marriage. Attempts are made to analyse the extent of observance of traditional norms of marriage as well as the attitudinal dimensions of the respondents towards various patterns of traditional marriage, and the extent of permissiveness to new trends in marriage. These again will be analysed for any relationship that there might exist between the different compositional structures of respondents' family and emerging trends in Hindu marriage.

Age of Marriage

To start with the age of marriage for boys and girls, we find that the injunctions laid down in the traditional Hindu philosophical and religious literature emphasized early marriage, specially that of girls. According to one formulation "if she does not marry before puberty the parents and eldest brother will go to hell" (Goode, *op. cit.*). Keeping a girl unmarried even after puberty was considered a sin of her parents who, in turn, were considered guilty of destruction of an 'embryo' every month (Kanan, 1963). These prescriptions in Brahmanical Hindu law books indicate prevailing values and attitudes in ancient India with regard to age of marriage for girls. Although in case of girls the rules were explicit and specific, yet in case of boys there was no religious prescription requiring them to marry early. However, "every Hindu writer agreed that the age of the bride must be less than that of the boy" (Prabhu, *op. cit.*). It appears that even an extremely wide gap between the ages of husband and wife was permissible. So far as the custom of marrying girls before puberty is concerned a number of reasons have been advanced by different scholars. According to Kapadia (*op. cit.*), since a girl had to make adjustments in the kin network of a large family it was necessary that she should be married quite early so that she might not be in a position to challenge the authority of the members of the family of her husband. According to Goode (*op. cit.,* 211), Hindu society viewed woman not only "as a temptation, but she was attributed with having great lusts. Thus for her own protection as well as protection of others she had to marry early due to the high regard for the chastity of woman, which was assured by her marriage, before she could lose her virginity or be suspected of having lost it" whatever might be the reasons this is definite that "this custom, began with high prestige, continued until the latter half of the 19th century" (Karve, *op. cit.*) and at the beginning of the British period, "almost all castes followed this practice" (Gangopadhayay, 1964:67). But, in more recent past, many factors contributed to end this practice. For example, the changed system of economy, giving birth to achieve occupations in place of ascribed and inherited occupations, required more time to be spent in education for getting new occupations. This exercised pressures for a higher age of marriage for men. In more recent times owing to difficulties in securing jobs youngmen are bound to marry at a later age. As an educated man would like to marry an educated girl, it is bound to raise the age of marriage even for girls. Dowry system, which ruined many families and crippled most, growing consciousness towards the consequences of early marriage on the health of girls and country's population are some of the other factors sensitizing people towards late age of marriage. In our own study, also, we find a tendency towards rise in the age of marriages.

To understand the growing influence of modern forces, cultural, social and economic, we have arranged our data to present a picture of the pattern prevailing at different periods of time. Table 7.1 highlights

Table 7.1: Mean age of marriage for males and females married during different period of time

	Categories of couples on the basis of their span of marriage	*Mean age for Males*	*Mean age for Females*
1.	For couples married during last 10 years	21.09	15.82
2.	For couples married during last 11 years to 20 years	20.20	15.75
3.	For couples married during last 21 to 30 years	19.84	14.68
4.	For couples married during last 31 to 40 years	19.07	14.25
5.	For couples married 41 years ago or even earlier than that	15.17	12.37

a clear shift in age of marriage of males and females from generation to generation rising up in the scale. The mean age of the marriage for the recently married couples (couples in category 1) is the highest and is higher than the ages traditionally regarded as appropriate. Since pre-pubertal marriage means marriage approximately before thirteen years of age, it is clear from Table 7.1 that pre-pubertal marriage was very popular some forty years back. Since then we find a radical departure from tradition. If we compare the mean ages specified for couples in category 1 with that of couples in categories 2, 3, 4 and 5, we find that at least during the last forty years the age of marriage is continuously rising. An analysis of the change in the mean ages of marriage during the last forty years, however, reveals the trend that although there has been a significant rise in the age of marriage of males, there is still a tendency not to delay the marriage of girls. This tendency is in turn an abject product of, the Hindu view and even practice that it is the foremost duty of parents to see that their daughter is married not too late, and to educate girls only to make them fit for marriage. This is not the position in case of boys,who have to be educated fully and to wait for years so that they may get a suitable career position.

If we consider the mean differences in the age of couples married during different periods of time (Table 7.2) we find that there existed and still exists a difference in the age of husband and wife and there has not been any clear narrowing or increase in the age differences of couples during different periods of time. Here it may be pointed out that in almost all the cases, except one in a Brahmin family and the other in a Rajput family, usually, the husband is older to wife. This desirability of the practice of selecting older grooms hints at the possible mentality among the Hindus that taking girl of equal age might

Table 7.2: Mean difference in the age of husband and wife married during different periods of time

	Categories of couples on the basis of their periods of marriage	*Mean differences in the age of husband and wife*
1.	For couples married during last 10 years	5.05
2.	For couples married during last 11 to 20 years	4.67
3.	For couples married during last 21 to 30 years	5.13
4.	For couples married during last 31 to 40 years	4.88
5.	For couples married 41 years ago or even earlier than that	5.62

imply a threat to the family system because it might militate against her position of subordination to her husband, as she might not accept the authority of either her in-laws or even her husband. Secondly, this may also be product of preferring occupationally settled and, therefore, older boys as grooms to girls. However, the tendency to marry a tender-age girl with an old groom does not appear to be an accepted trend. Comparing the behavioural propensity with the attitudinal dimensions we find that respondents exhibit higher approbation for late marriage for both boys and girls. A comparison of the mean age of marriage specified by respondents with the prevailing trend in this sphere as reflected by the mean ages of marriage of recently married couples (couples married during last ten years), however, shows that there is a slightly more marked trend in the gradual departure from tradition of marrying girls at lower age (Table 7.3). With the rising uncertainty of the job-availability to youngman the girl's family would also be required to wait for a considerable period of time. The analysis of the specification of age at marriage for boys and girls reveals the tendency of maintaining difference in the ages of bride and bridegroom and this practice occupies approximately the same range of permissiveness as was reflected in the pattern of observance of age difference in the case of recently married couple. But the fact that none of our respondents preferred a bride older to the boy highlights the tendency that Hindus are still inclined to favour and support superior positions to males by preferring younger wives to them.

Table 7.3 : Mean age of marriage preferred for boys and girls

Age preferred for boys (Means)	Age preferred for girls (Means)
22.5	17.3

Before we proceed to analyse the specified ages of marriage by families of different compositional forms. It would not be out of place to mention that the practice of marrying boys and girls at an early age was conducive to maintenance of the traditional joint family. Because the fabric of relationship as operating in a joint family requires complete submissiveness and docility on the part of a new bride, if she was quite grown up at the time of her marriage, it would be difficult to mould her to suit the environment of the new family and she would become a source of irritation and tension for the entire family. Due to this fact and our presumption that the joint family should be more conservative than the traditional family behaviour, it can be hoped that the joint family would show less approval to the new trend in marriage characterised by late marriage and emphasis on the equality in the age of couples. But if we analyse Table 7.4 which gives the mean ages of marriage considered appropriate by the heads of the families of different compositions we find that the differences in the ages as specified by the corresponding groups of the joint and nuclear families are very narrow. It is clear that respondents belonging to both types of families are more or less equally sensitised to the harmful effects of early marriage. The family composition does not appear to be significantly related to the age of marriage specified by the respondents.

Table 7.4 : Mean of the ages preferred for marriage of boys and girls and the family type

Type of family	*Mean of the Age preferred*	
	For boys	*For girls*
Nuclear family	22.5	17.2
Joint family	22.8	17.4

Inter-Caste Marriage

After analysing the changes in the age of marriage, we now intend to examine other important trends of Hindu marriage. One important feature of Hindu marriage has been the observance of rules of endogamy and exogamy. In fact, the selection of marriage partner is never free in the sense that any man has got the freedom to marry any woman. Among both, the savage and the civilized, it is subject to a number of rules specifying whom one may marry or may not marry. Everywhere some bans and bars exist on the pattern of the selection of marriage. Rules of endogamy and exogamy are the most important rules governing marriage. To elaborate them, while the rule of endogamy defines everywhere an outer circle, out of which marriage is definitely banned, that of exogamy draws an inner circle within which no marriage is permitted. Hindus have always instead on caste endogamy, upon which the maintenance of the caste system depended to a large extent. The traditional Hindu view is that every member is to marry a girl belonging to the same caste. It is held that "the rule of endogamy expresses a desire to maintain racial purity or occupational monopoly or economic privileges or group solidarity of caste" (Mathur, 1964: 47). In practice rigorous observation of this rule was the only course open to Hindus The violation of this ritually sanctioned rule was punished by excommunication from the caste meaning great hardships to the deviant.

However, enactment of legislative measures in pre-independent as well as in post-independent India to invalidate the importance of caste in marriage, greater exposure to secular and modern ideas, increased education have rendered the situation altogether different. " Not only has the prevalence of inter-caste marriage become considerable, but even the difficulties, the inter-caste marriage couples have to face, have become comparatively quite mild" (*op. cit.,* vii). Thus, the present era represents a changed spectrum with regard to the rule of endogamy. In this background we propose to examine the attitudes of the members of different types of families with regard to the practice of inter-caste marriage. With this end in view we will analyse the extent of respondents reaction towards *pratiloma* and *anuloma* types of inter-caste marriages in a hypothetical situation when their (i) boys and (ii) girls are parties to such marriages. However, before analysing the responses it is worth mentioning that, according to the Brahmin law givers, the marriage of a higher status male with a low status female is called *anuloma* (in consonance with *dharma*) and the marriage between a man of lower status and a woman of higher status is called *pratiloma*. It is said that though the *anuloma* marriages (hypergamous marriages) were not common and though they meant deprivation of certain privileges to the progeny born of such marriages, yet these were sanctioned. It is traditionally accepted as in consonance with *dharma*. In the past hypergamous and hypogamous marriages were of the nature of inter-caste marriages between families of different strata. In fact, this gives birth to the dowry system. Later on, when there was extension of such marriages outside the caste, this term began to be identified mostly with reference to inter-caste marriages. We have also used these terms in the context of inter-caste marriage.

It appears from Table 7.5 that in both types of families hypergamous marriage is preferred by the parents of brides than by the parents of grooms, and *pratiloma* marriage appears to be more favoured among the parents of bridegrooms than by the parents of brides. This corroborates the possibility pointed out by Kanan (*ibid*). However, the fact that only a small percentage of respondents in both types of family favours inter-caste marriage proves that there is a wide gap between the legislative measures, secular environment and modernization, on the one hand, and permissiveness and encouragement to inter-caste marriage, on the other. This trend is due to the problems faced in inter-caste marriage and due to the positive rewards to be gained by inter-caste marriage, there is little encouragement to inter-caste marriage so log suitable partners can be found within own caste. However, a comparison of the percentage of the respondents in the nuclear family, favouring inter-caste marriage, with those from the joint family shows that both as parents of males as well as of females, the joint family respondents show less approval for hypergamous marriage as well as hypogamous marriage than the nuclear family. Of course, in the case of hypogamous marriage as parents of females there is very little difference between the attitudes of the respondents of different families, yet broadly the data as contained in Table 7.5 goes to highlight the traditional and conservative nature of the joint family. The percentages of those favouring inter-caste marriage increases as the composition of family changes from joint to nuclear.

Table 7.5: Reaction of parents towards inter-caste marriage by family types

Situations	*Percentage of persons encouraging inter-caste marriage*	
	Nuclear family	*Joint family*
1. When a boy of the family is a party to hypergamous marriage	10.5	4.3
2. When a girl of the family is a party to hypogamous marriage	9.1	5.1
3. When a boy of the family is a party to hypogamous marriage	13.1	10.1
4. When a girl of the family is a party to hypogamous marriage	6.1	6.5

However, if we compare the attitudinal dimensions of the respondents with the actual behavioural propensity we find that in their attitudes some respondents might be ready to breakthrough the rules of caste endogamy, but when the question of actual practice comes the picture appears to be even more conservative. Out of 160 respondents only two cases are such where the couples belong to two different castes. We describe the details of these cases below as narrated by the respondents themselves:

Case 1

"I belong to a Bhumihar landed family. My family owned zamindari in past. We lived in a joint family. As a student of the post-graduate class, I developed intimacy with a girl of a Brahmin family. We liked each other intimately. When we decided to get married we knew that my father would not like it because of two factors. First, this would have meant that in future there would be great difficulty in the marriage of my younger siblings particularly my sisters and, secondly, this would have implied an immediate loss of Rs. 35,000 to my family, which would have come to my family by way of dowry. I knew this also that since the girl belonged to a caste different and higher to mine, the other family would also not allow it. As a result without informing anybody we registered a civil marriage. After a few days I informed my parents as well as my in-laws. On receipt of my letter my father wrote a letter to my father-in-law requesting him to see that the union is broken. My father wrote in the letter even this that since I would not get any share in the joint family it would mean hardships for the girl also. As a result my father-in-law came within few days and took his daughter to his home town. The girl was rebuked by her family members and they decided to re-marry her with a Brahmin boy. She was also told that since any resistance on her part would result in legal proceedings against the family, therefore, in the interest of the family and her parents, she should keep mum and co-operate with whatever was done. She was also told that there was every likelihood that I shall be deprived of the financial assistance for continuing my study by my father and living with me would bring her only troubles. In two or three days my legally wedded bride was taken from Bihar to Madhya Pradesh for a second marriage. All the time my wife was too shocked to do anything or to speak anything. But, at last, good sense prevailed and on the intervention of some relatives my father-in-law gave up the idea to re-marry her. They returned to their home town and the girl was formally sent back to me. Gradually my father also gave up all resistance. But this was not all. My family still suffered a lot of troubles at times, particularly our castemen were not prepared to dine with me. But due to the traditional respect and authority commanded by my grandfather, this problem too was amicably settled and my family was not outcasted".

Case 2

" In her youth, after becoming widow, my mother eloped with a man of Kurmi caste of the same village and settled at Patna. Since my father was Kurmi and my mother was a Kanhar I could get bride in Kurmi only. But when I grew up and reached the mar-

> riageable age, I found that no Kurmi was prepared to marry his daughter with me. Ultimately when I was twenty-five years of age, some friends of mine informed me that there was girl who was kidnapped from her village by somebody. After living with the man for few days she had cunningly left him and now was working as a maid in a richman's house. I sent my mother there to inquire from her if she was ready to marry. On her consenting to the proposal, in a temple I put vermilion on her forehead and she was accepted as my bride. Those who know my history, know well why I have married her. But this was the only course open to me if I was to be married at all."

On the basis of these cases no generalization can be made, yet they illustrate certain peculiarities of inter-caste marriages and these are noted below:

First, it appears that in inter-caste marriage initiative for selection of a partner solely rests with the parties themselves with or without anybody's assistance. Secondly, inter-caste marriage appears to be the product of development of intimacy between parties or the incapacity of some outcasted man. Thirdly, it also shows that a boy or a girl of a traditional family revolting against the rule of caste endogamy is not easily taken back into the family-fold. There are a great many difficulties. But if one of the parties to an inter-caste marriage is a progeny born out of a previous inter-caste marriage, then he is helped by his family members to secure a marriage partner. To end the discussion on inter-caste marriage it is clear that so far as the rule of endogamy is concerned it is still rigorously adhered to, with the only difference that whereas formerly inter-caste marriage was not even thought of, today at least some persons, are prepared to revolt against this tradition. Yet the ideological support to this new trend in marriage is far ahead of its actual practice in life.

Arranged Marriage Versus Love Match

Besides its endogamous nature, another traditional feature of Hindu marriage is that it is characterised by arranged marriages. In fact, arranged marriage was the system for all other family patterns characterising Hindu society and freedom of choice in marriage was quite unthinkable. Since marriage was regarded as an alliance between two families, parents were morally obliged to find mates for their children and the children in turn used to accept the decisions of the parents. " Love between husband and wife was the result of marriage in Hindu view, not the prelude to it" (Tagore, 1920).

The arranged nature of Hindu marriage was practically conducive to the maintenance of the joint family system and the caste system. So that the new marriage partner must have a complete assimilation with large kin-network, the family elders controlled the choice. With a view to study the extent of permissiveness to marriages based on romantic love by the partners, we asked the respondents as to which they consider better (1) love marriage (based on the romantic love of the marriage partners) or (ii) a marriage arranged by parents and which is not based on romantic love of the marriage partners. On examining Table 7.6 containing the responses with regard to this question we find that, in spite of the progressive penetration of liberal ideas in the country, love marriage has not yet popularised with our respondents and only a small proportion of respondents is in favour of breaking tradition whereas a big majority prefers the tradition of arranged marriage. It is also clear from Table 7.6 that so far as permissiveness to love marriage is concerned, the family type is a major differentiating factor. Though, both in the case of joint family and nuclear family, a larger percentage of respondents are for preservation of the patterns of arranged marriage, the percentage is higher in case of the joint family

Table 7.6 : Family type and permissiveness to love marriage

Statement	*Percentage of persons saying 'yes'*	
	Nuclear family	*Joint family*
Love marriage is better to arranged marriage	19.2	8.6

than the nuclear family. This is but natural because in the nuclear family the husband-wife relation is "the pivot of the structure" requiring personal compatibility of husband and wife which is not the position in the case of the joint family system, where marital choice is supposed to be subordinate to group ends. A comparison of the actualities in performance with attitudinal dimensions of respondents, so far as love marriages are concerned, reveals a big gap between the two. In all 160 families studied, only three cases of love marriage have been reported. Out of these one belongs to the domain of inter-caste marriage and has been dealt in detail while discussing the cases of inter-caste marriage. The other two which are intra-caste in nature and discussed below quoting the respondents themselves:

Case 1

" I was a member of a traditional joint family of Rajputs. My father had complete authority over the family. While as a college student, I fell in love with a sister of one of my Rajput friends. When I proposed to marry the girl, after a little resistance, the girl's people agreed.. Yet I did not disclose these things to my parents out of fear. When the marriage date drew nearer, I disclosed my decisions to my parents. So far as I think this opposition was due mainly to two main reasons. First, I had challenged my father's authority to negotiate my marriage. As my father told "due to your conduct I cannot make appearance in the village. You have shown to everybody that I have no authority over you". Secondly, because I was going to engaged with a girl of my own choice, this meant loss of a large amount of money, which my family could have easily obtained by way of dowry. Now since the family of the bride wanted solemnization of the marriage in accordance with the traditional pattern, I had to prepare for the marriage procession without the help of the angry kinsmen of my family. Consequently my marriage party consisted only of my friends. When I returned with my wife to my family nobody spoke to her. I had warned her in advance of this possibility. While this type of thing continued, once my mother fell ill. This was a God-sent opportunity to my wife to demonstrate her qualities. She nursed my mother day and night. The services rendered by her won the heart of my father and gradually she became the dearest daughter-in-law of my parents.

Case 2

"I was a member of a Rajput nuclear family. My father was a well-placed government officer. Just by the side of my father's quarters, there was residence of another government officer who was also Rajput by caste. In the course of time I developed some intimacy with a daughter of that Rajput officer. I determined to marry the girl because she was educated and was very amiable in nature. But there was one difficulty. This was my father's desire to marry me with a daughter of a big zamindar. However, when I got sufficient courage, I communicated my decision to my father. Expectantly the initial reaction was of anger and disapproval. Yet perhaps because he was an educated man and perhaps because the bride's family was also not inferior to that of mine, my father reconciled and my marriage was solemnized in a manner which was not different from the patterns of celebrations of an arranged marriage."

The hindu family seems to be greatly oriented towards the view that arranging marriage is the exclusive prerogative of the parents and if a son does it at his own, it is a potent source of threat to the family. The opposition to love marriage (as apparent from the cases) appears to be, first, due to rigorous acceptance of traditionalities in marriage. Secondly, since marriage is considered by Hindus to be a relation between two families, allowing romantic love to become the basis of marriage might mean choosing a girl which might not belong to a traditionally reputed family, thus damaging the reputation of the family concerned. Thirdly, opposition to such marriage from the side of groom's family is also due to loss of money, through dowry. Particularly for such grooms; families, which have to incur huge expenditure as dowry for girls, love marriage resulting in loss of money becomes a source of strain. However, partners to inter-caste love marriages seem to be more easily reincorporated into the web of family relationship after an initial period of hostility than the partners of inter-caste marriages who suffer numerous troubles.

Participation by a Man in the Selection of his Mate

The lower range of permissiveness to romantic love as the bases of marriage does not imply that the marriage partners are completely denied any participation in the selection of their life partners. In fact, from our data it is quite apparent that, perhaps in a bid to adjust itself with the changes in society, the Hindu family is permitting more and more participation in the selection of life-partners to individuals. To study the extent of degree of participation allowed, the schedule contained a question asking the respondent to spell the extent to which participation is allowed to a boy of the family for the selection of his bride. The varying extent of participation has been delineated under three categories, viz, (i) full participation, (2) little participation (by way of seeking opinion of the boy or by letting him have a look at his prospective bride or her photograph), and (3) No participation.

Table 7.7 : Degree of participation allowed to men in selection of their mates

	*Extent of participation**	*Percentage of families permitting different degrees of participation*
1.	Complete participation	25.6
2.	Limited participation	41.5
3.	No participation	33.1

* If a boy is allowed only to see the girl or her photograph to suggest his approval or disapproval of the girl, his participation in the selection of girl has been called limited. On the other hand if he participates in every detail of the settlement of his marriage, then he has been considered here as fully participating in the selection of his bride.

It appears from Table 7.7 that very conservative families deny any participation to boys in the selection process. But they are not in majority. At the same time those allowing full participation are also in minority. It can be said that a middle path has been adopted by the larger number of families. In other words, as a compromise to the old practice of keeping arrangement of marriage away from the partners (as apparent in the case of men) with the rising desire of the individuals to get more

Table 7.8 : Family type and degree of participation allowed to males in selection of mates

	Extent of participation	*Percentage of families permitting different degrees of participation*	
		Nuclear family	*Joint family*
1.	Full participation	28.9	17.4
2.	Limited participation	41.2	41.3
3.	No participation	29.9	41.3

and more involvement in the selection of their brides a majority of families are inclined to attach importance to participation by the boy whose marriage is being settled. If we proceed still further to analyse our data to compare the positions prevalent in the nuclear as well as the joint family, we find (see Table 7.8) that so far as the percentage of families allowing only a little participation to man in the selection of his mate is concerned, there is a similarity in the practices of the nuclear and joint families. But it is also revealed from Table 7.8 that the nuclear families are more inclined to full participation to the individual than the joint families. Similarly in joint families there is greater conservativeness is not allowing any participation to men than nuclear family. The trend, therefore, is definitely on the increase of allowing participation of men in the process of selection of their life partners, particularly more in the case of the nuclear families.

Matching the Horoscopes

Another traditional feature of Hindu marriage is the great premium on matching the horoscopes of marriage partners before final settlement. This flows out of the belief among Hindus on fate. The belief in horoscope shows a faith in the irrevocability of destiny. "Parents today often insist on it in order to free their own conscience from the heavy

Table 7.9 Practice of matching horoscopes by different types of families

Type of family	*Percentage of families which match horoscopes before marriage*
Nuclear family	75.4
Joint family	86.0

responsibility of choosing bridegrooms", (Brahman; in Ross; *op.cit,* 254). So far as the matching of horoscopes is concerned our data show that as many as 78.1 per cent of the families consider matching of horoscopes as a necessary prerequisite to the settlement of marriage. A comparison of the extent of observance of the practice of matching horoscopes by different types of family shows greater conservatism in joint families as compared to nuclear families (Table 7.9). How much importance is attached to matching of horoscopes by different types of family is illustrated in the following cases narrated by the respondents or other members of the families studied.

Case 1

"I belong to a joint family. My father being an ardent believer in horoscope, whenever any party came to negotiate my marriage, he used to first demand the horoscope of the girl. As soon as it was available to him, he used to take it personally to an astrologer in whom he had great faith. In this way not less than 20 parties came and many offered handsome dowry to me, but since their horoscopes were rejected by the astrologer, every offer was refused. Ultimately I was married to a girl whose horoscope tallied with mine, even though my father did not get very handsome dowry for me".

Case 2

"When I was being married my family was nuclear in character. An astrologer told father that my due to peculiar nature of my horoscope, great precaution was to be taken in my marriage, so far as matching of horoscopes is concerned. Many offers came, but all were gradually rejected. I waited for two years, but could not speak anything. After two years, on the advice of the astrologer, I was married with a girl whose horoscope matched with mine. I must tell, that my parents were so anxious to get me married with a girl of matching horoscope that they did not care even for the physical appearance of the girl. Though my conjugal life is happy now, in the beginning I was very much disappointed at the choice of my parents".

Case 3

"As a head of a nuclear family my father, who was a high Government Officer, arranged the marriage of my sister without giving any importance to the practice of matching horoscopes. It so happened that within 15 days of the marriage my father died of heart attack. Many persons, including my mother, even now believe that it was the bad effect of the union which took my father's life. As the astrologer later on told us, the nature of the horoscopes of my sister and brother-in-law were such that a marriage of the two was bound to cause the death either of my father or one of the couples.

Case 4

"My father had two daughters. At that time my family was joint. So far as marriage of one of my sisters was concerned, a groom having matching horoscope was easily found but in the case of other sister, my father visited at least twenty places. When the desired choice was available, he paid a heavy dowry to make his parents agree to the marriage proposal".

All these cases point out that the Hindu faith in horoscope and, therefore, destiny is deep-set and fear of destiny is not a fact to be ignored.

Criteria in Selection of Spouses

In all cases of marriage there are bound to be certain abstract preference for selection of mates. Therefore, an analysis of pattern of marriage as prevalent in the society would be incomplete without a study of criterion of selection. As such, the schedule included a question asking respondents to mention whether they considered family status, education, economic position and physical attractiveness of the mate to be important factors in case they have to (1) select a wife for a boy of the family and (2) select a husband for a girl of the family. The selection of these attributes was done after analysing the types of responses obtained to a free response question while the schedule was being pre-tested. The responses obtained in the final study, given in Table 7.10 show that these attributes in majority cases appear to be widely acceptable criteria, both for the selection of a wife or a husband. Over and above these attributes two respondents mentioned personal compatibility of mates as criterion of selection, in two other cases temperament and character were considered as desirable trait for a bride.

Table 7.10 : Preference of respondents of different family types with regard to certain specified attributes in selection of mate partners

Attributes	*Percentage of respondents approving the attributes*			
	In the selection of bride		*In the selection of bridegroom*	
	Nuclear family	*Joint family*	*Nuclear family*	*Joint family*
1. Khandan (Social status of family)	97.3	100	90.3	91.0
2. Education	90.3	81.6	92.9	89.0
3. Economic position	78.2	63.0	94.7	93.0
4. Attractiveness	94.7	93.4	70.1	67.3

A close look at Table 7.10 reveals that so far as selection of bride is concerned, *Khandan* appears to be the most important factor getting approval as a desirable trait by largest number of respondents. Attractiveness of the girl appears to be the next important factor while education and economic position of the bride or her family getting third and fourth positions respectively. In case of selection of husband, although his *Khandan* is considered to be an important trait yet the most important place is given to the economic position of the boy or his family. A lesser importance to the *Khandan*, so far as the selection of a husband is concerned, may be appreciated in the light of the limitations imposed upon bride's family in selection of husband on account of ruinous dowry system and stiff competition in finding a suitable match. Physical appearance of the husband appears to be a less important factor when compared to its position with regard to selection of bride. Thus, on the one hand, in the selection of wife greater emphasis is placed on traditional traits represented by *Khandan* and attractiveness than the attributes of modernity represented by education, on the other hand, in the case of selection of husbands, education and economic position get wider acceptance to traditionality (*Khandan*).

If we try to examine the differences in the pattern of preferences as reflected by the responses of the joint and nuclear families respondents we find that in case of the joint family, there is not even a single respondent who does not favour *Khandan* as a desirable trait. But the extent of performances of the nuclear family for *Khandan* speaks of at least a slant tendency towards overlooking this traditional point of emphasis. In the same way, educated wife is more a preference of the nuclear family than the joint family. This attribute finds larger favour with nuclear family respondents prone to modernity than the tradition-prone joint family respondents. There is practically negligible difference in the extent of preference of the joint and nuclear families respondents so far as attractiveness of the husband is concerned. In case of selection of a bridegroom the only marked difference found in the case of the different family types lies in the fact that in case of education, nuclear family appears to be more proximate to modernity than joint family.

Seeing Girl before Marriage

Another change in the traditional marriage pattern is visible in the practice of inspecting the prospective bride before marriage by the members of the bridegroom's family. In case of the families studied, we find that in as many as 74.3 per cent of families the practice of seeing the bride for marriage is prevalent. It is day-by-day becoming a necessary prelude to settlement of marriage. To quote a head of a joint family:

> "Since seeing the girl before marriage might mean her rejection, I had thought that for the selection of my daughter-in-law I would never press the other side for showing the girl before marriage. As such when my eldest son was being married we did not go to see the girl, but from other sources I got satisfactory information with regard to the girl and her family. As a matter of fact, now I feel that I have been cheated. My eldest daughter-in-law is rather ugly. I have now determined that I would never finalise any marriage negotiation unless the bride is personally seen by some members of my family."

Thus it is clear that in order to be fully satisfied with the beauty of the girl. Now there is a feeling that the girl must be "shown before she is finally approved to be taken in the new family":

To quote the head of nuclear family:

> "I think that being father of a girl in India is a sin. Since my daughter is not beautiful and is not well educated. I was very afraid at the time of her marriage. Because once a girl is rejected by any family where her marriage is being negotiated this becomes an obstacle in her way of marriage even in some other family. So when every thing was settled and my daughter was now to be seen, I arranged for it in a Dharmashala, without telling anybody anything. I am glad that my daughter was accepted by the other party. But at that time one thing irritated me greatly that in this process one of the ladies who had assembled there asked my daughter to read few sentences from a book, especially brought for the purpose. But now I think that they were right because often we hear that some groom family is cheated due to the exaggerated narration of bride's qualities by the bride's parents."

In some cases the girl is seen by women related to the bridegroom's family, in others by both men and women of the family. In order to see that in how many families there is a practice to allow even the bridegroom to see the bride before her marriage our schedule incorporated a question seeking to elicit that information. Our data show that only in 31.9 per cent of the families, which allow inspection of bride, the practice of seeing girl before marriage by bridegroom also is prevalent. A comparison of the difference between the joint and the

Table 7.11 : Family type and the practice of allowing boys to see the mate before marriage

Family type	*Percentage of family where bridegroom goes to see the bride*
Nuclear family	36.7
Joint family	22.5

nuclear families so far as the prevalence of this practice is concerned shows that the practice finds greater currency in the nuclear families than the joint families, once again establishing that the nuclear family is more expose to the new trends in marriage showing greater approval to these trends than the joint family (Table 7.11).

Divorce

We have noted earlier that the Hindu marriage is not a civil contract, it is a sacrament. It is considered to be a life-long union of partners. Besides this, being union of souls, is ordained that they would be brought together whenever they take birth. Thus marriage is considered to be a pre-ordained relationship between partners. All these go to emphasize that the relationship between husband and wife is indissoluble. But from this it would be wrong to assume that Hindu law books did not sanction divorce. The discussion on the scriptural position regarding divorce as presented by Prabhu (*op. cit.*), shows that divorce or dissolution of marriage was permitted by the Dharmashastra but this was permitted in cases which were highly exceptional. Yet, particularly among lower and scheduled caste Hindus divorce and separation have been widely prevalent in the past also. In contemporary India there is now a legal provision for divorce. The legislation raised a storm and it was apprehended that acceptance of this measure by all castes would destroy the web of relationship operating in family. An analysis of the responses to the question regarding the permissiveness of divorce, as contained in Table 7.12 shows that the acceptors of the provision of divorce are very few.

Table 7.12 : Family type and permissiveness to divorce

Statement	*Percentage of respondents saying 'yes'*	
	Nuclear family	*Joint family*
Divorce should be permitted	16.6	8.6

Table 7.12 further reveals that joint family respondents are generally more conservative as compared to those of nuclear families insofar as permissiveness to the provisions of divorce is concerned.

In actual practice we observed only two cases of dissolution of marriage, that too among the Chamars. In one of the two cases the chastity of the woman was doubted and in another case the woman herself left her husband on account of his being physically invalid. These two happened without taking resort to any legal machinery. In short, we can say that "divorce has not yet gained general acceptance, and that many conflicts will centre around this crucial aspect of the marriage pattern in the years to come" (Ross, *op. cit.*, 275).

While studying the different dimensions of the institution of marriage, first we found that during the last forty years the age of marriage of boys and girls is rising. However, the tendency of late marriage is more marked in the case of boys than girls. The tendency to maintain difference in the age of husband and wife still persists. However, both types of family are more or less equally sensitized to the harmful effects of early marriage and the family type does not appear to be significantly related to the age of marriage specified by the respondent. So far as permissiveness to inter-caste marriage is concerned, there appears to be a wide gap between the legislative measures, secular environment and modernization on the one hand and permissiveness and encouragement to inter-caste marriages on the other. There appears to be little encouragement to inter-caste marriages so long. Suitable partners can easily be obtained within own caste. Analysing the desirability of *pratiloma* and *anuloma* marriages we find that the trend of desirability is in the predicted direction-parents of bride favouring *anuloma* marriage in larger percentage than the parents of bridegroom and vice versa. We also find that in their attitudes some respondents might be ready to breakthrough the rule of caste endogamy but in practice only a negligible number of respondents has come forward. So far as family type is concerned, joint family shows less approval to intercaste marriage than nuclear family. Love marriage has not yet gained general acceptance with our respondents and only a small proportion of respondents is for violation of tradition and a big majority of respondents prefers the traditional arrangement. Family type appears to be a major differentiating factor so far as permissiveness to love marriage is concerned. Nuclear family respondents are in larger proportion in favour of love marriages than the joint family respondents. In a bid to adjust itself with the changes in society, the Hindu family is permitting more and more participation in selection of life partners to the men. The data also revealed that the nuclear family is giving more latitude to members than the joint family so far as participation in selection of life partners by men is concerned. The practice of matching horoscopes is prevalent among larger number of respondents. There appears to be greater conservation in matching horoscopes by the joint family than by the nuclear family. Social status of the family, education of the mate, economic position and physical attractiveness are important attributes emphasized in the selection of life-partners. In the case of selection of bridegrooms, social status of the family is the most important point of emphasis, and, in the case of selection of bride, this position has been given to attractiveness of the girl. The traditional points of emphasis are being overlooked by nuclear family respondents in larger percentage than those of joint family. The practice of seeing girl before marriage is found more in the case of nuclear families than in case of joint families. The nuclear family shows more favourable attitudes towards divorce than the joint family.

8

FAMILY AND CLASS

SOCIAL DIFFERENCE in the status of an individual or a group is a general problem and is found in every society. In primitive as well as contemporary societies, Western as well as non-Western countries, social inequality had existed in the past as well as exists in the present."Recently writers on aspects of social stratification have been thinking of social status in terms of a continuum of societies. At one end are societies in which the status of the individual tends to remain fixed for life, at the other are societies in which the opportunity for advancement of status of individual is recognized and even encouraged. In other words, at one end is the caste system, at the other the so-called 'open class system'" (Cox, 1959 : 298). Of the two, the first (the caste system) has been "one of the exclusive characteristics of the Indian society since early ages" (Paranjpe, 1970:1). Even at present, caste is an important and sacrosanct institution in India, particularly with Hindus. The Hindu society is a castes ridden society. It is the bed-rock of Hindu life. The division of the Hindu society into groups, based on the ritual concepts of purity and pollution, has been responsible for separating each of these groups on the basis of custom, occupation and food practices. Each individual is expected to conform to the rules, norms and customs prescribed by the caste. In fact, prior to the advent of industrialization and urbanization, caste was the main and the most powerful and important factor regulating the status, behaviour and value system of Hindus.

With the advent of industrialization, economic and industrial forces began to impinge on social structure. The social barriers appropriate for a stable type of economy became week. "The history of the industrialization of many countries shows that one of the fundamental changes in social structure which takes place with the coming of the modern industrial age is that the rigidly structured strata of the feudal age gradually give way to an open class society" (Ghurye, 1952 : 150). Considering the background of recent social changes, it is often mentioned that the system of caste is fading. It is said that caste barriers are being removed by the forces of urbanization and industrialization characterised by greater physical mobility, secularised orientation, changed cultural environments, etc. There has been the birth of a system of dispersed inequalities in the place of cumulative inequalities. Now, in the place of caste, family and individual became the important factors determining the social and economic status of an individual. The hold of caste in many areas of social life tends to be weakened. For example, education is no longer the monopoly of a particular caste. Everybody is now legally free to choose his own style of life. Fitness for any occupation is not determined by the birth of individual in any particular caste, but by his own achievements. Due to all these, new social groupings replacing caste have emerged. This is the opinion of one class of scholars. But there are others who say that class system has not sounded the death knell of caste system and, "in spite of changes in some of its external features, the caste system has retained most of its essential functions" (Paranjpe, *op. cit.*, 1). In this chapter it will be our endeavour to examine the influence of these traditional and modern bases of stratification on the behavioural propensity as well as the attitudinal dimensions of the respondents of different types of the families studied. In this way we will try to discover the varying importance of caste and class separately for different types of families. For this purpose we have chosen from our data at least one item from each aspect to see the extent to which class and caste work as variables. From the data on marriage we have selected three items. The selection of these items are purely accidental and without any bias. By class we mean the various economic strata in which families of the present studies are placed.

Handling of Money

From the data on 'Division of labour' we have analysed the question of handling of money in the family. If we relate the deviation from role conventionality in this duty with caste and economic background of different types of families, we find that caste does not play a very significant role in determining the deviation from role conventionality.

Table 8.1(a) : Deviation from role conventionality with regard to handling of money related to family type and caste

Caste	*Percentage of families deviating from role conventionality*	
	Nuclear	*Joint*
Upper	22.8	13.0
Lower	14.0	21.7

Table 8.1(a) shows that in nuclear families, upper caste families are more inclined to deviate from role conventionality than the lower caste families. But in case of joint family the picture is reverse. Thus we can say that caste is not a significant variable, strong enough to affect deviation from role conventionality in all types of families. Now if we correlate the economic status of the families with deviation from role conventionality, we find that there is a significant correspondence between deviation from role conventionality in different types of families and their economic status.

Table 8.1 (b) : Deviation from role conventionality in families of different compositions and economic statuses

Income Groups	*Percentage of the families deviating from role conventionality*	
	Nuclear	*Joint*
1. Families having monthly income of Rs. 300 or below	13.1	14.2
2. Families having monthly income between Rs. 301 and 800	28.9	15.7
3. Families having monthly income of Rs. 801 and above	14.8	23.0

Table 8.1(b) shows that the lowest income group in all types of families is less inclined to allow their women to handle money as compared to the higher income groups. The high income families appear to be more susceptible to the forces of urbanization and industrialization compelling the high income families to deviate from the traditional allocated pattern of role performance.

The Relationship between Husband and Wife

We have observed earlier that there are certain joint families where husband and wife are not allowed even to talk freely to each other. On analyzing the caste background of such families we find that caste is an important variable determining the possibility of free talk between husband and wife.

Table 8.2(a) : Castewise percentage of the Joint Families where husband and wife do not talk to each other freely

Caste	*Percentage of families*
Upper	17.3
Lower	34.6

Table 8.2(a) reveals that the joint families from upper castes are more progressive than lower caste joint families in permitting free talk between husband and wife. The lower caste families appear to be more traditional. While the internalization of traditional values has made the lower caste families rather rigid, the internalization of nuclear values has led the upper caste to be less rigid with regard to the aspect of husband-wife interaction pattern. On the other hand the economic status of these families shows that although those in the highest income brackets are not averse to free talk between husband and wife yet, at the same time, it is also clear that every rise in income does not lead to egalitarian pattern in husband-wife interaction (see Table 8.2b).

Table 8.2(b) : Classwise classification of the Joint Families where husband and wife cannot talk freely with each other

	Income Group	*Percentage of families*
1.	Families having monthly income of Rs. 300 or below	35.7
2.	Families having monthly income between Rs. 301 and 800	36.8
3.	Families having monthly income of Rs. 801 or above	0

Thus a comparison of the findings of two Tables [8.2(a), 8.2(b)] reveals that caste is distinctly related to husband wife interaction pattern while there is not a positive and continuous correspondence between rise in income and behavioural pattern of the family.

Decision-making in the Selection of Bride

Of all the spheres selected for the study of decision-making, in the sphere of selection of bride women have been mentioned to be the final and most effective decision-maker by the largest number of respondents. If we analyse the caste composition of the families where women are the final and most effective decision-makers with regard to selection of bride, we find that women of lower castes are more dominant than those of upper castes so far as the joint families are concerned. Whereas in the case of the nuclear families the picture is just the reverse [See Table 8.3(a)].

Table 8.3(a) : Caste and type of families where women are final decision-maker with regard to selection of bride

Caste	*Percentage of families where women are final decision-makers*	
	Nuclear	*Joint*
Upper	16.6	26.3
Lower	15.0	33.3

However, analysis of the economic status of such families shows that lowest income groups are less inclined to accept women as final decision-makers than high income groups. This is true in case of both types of the families ([See Table 8.3(b)].

Here it is also apparent that with every increase in income, cases where females are final decision-maker do not increase.

Education versus Employment

While dealing with 'work and family', on the basis of a hypothetical question, we had tried to delineate the families whose heads are more oriented to employment than to education. Here we analyse the caste and class compositions of such families which are more oriented to employment than to education. If we look into Table [8.4(a)] we will find that caste does not affect the attitudinal dimensions of respondents in a particular direction. In nuclear families, upper caste respondents seem to be less impatient for employment than the lower caste respondents. But in case of joint families the situation becomes exactly opposite. However, if we analyse the economic status of the respondents favouring immediate gratification instead of deferred gratification, we find that there is an inverse relationship between high income on the one hand and orientation towards deferred gratification on the other [Table 8.4 (b)].

Table 8.3 (b) : Economic status and type of families where women are final decision-making centres with regard to selection of bride

	Income group	*Percentage of families where women are final decision-makers*	
		Nuclear	*Joint*
1.	Families having monthly income of Rs. 300 or below	9.2	30.7
2.	Families having monthly income between Rs. 301 and 800	28.1	66.6
3.	Families having monthly income of Rs. 801 or above	25.0	36.3

Table 8.4(a) : Caste, family type and preference for employment over education

Statement	*Percentage of respondents saying 'yes'*			
	Upper caste		*Lower caste*	
	Nuclear	*Joint*	*Nuclear*	*Joint*
If the student is brilliant and wants to continue his studies and he is also getting a job, should he give up study	19.2	52.1	36.7	43.4

Table 8.4 (b) : Class, family type and preference for employment over education

Statement	*Percentage of Respondents saying 'yes'*					
	Nuclear family Families having monthly income			*Joint family Families having monthly income*		
	Rs. 300 or below	*Between Rs. 301 and 800*	*Above Rs. 800*	*Rs. 300 or below*	*Between Rs. 301 and 800*	*Above Rs. 800*
If the student is brilliant and wants to study and he is also getting a job, should he give up study	36.2	15.7	14.2	57.1	52.6	30.7

From Table 8.4(b) we find that with a change from lower economic status to higher economic status, the percentage of respondents preferring job in place of education for a brilliant student declines. This is quite natural, because economic factor is the permissive factor for continuing study. Until and unless a head of the family has sufficient resources at its disposal, he cannot be oriented to deferred gratification. Thus we can say that class appears to be more powerful variable than caste in compelling respondent to choose between a job and continuation of education.

Practice of Matching Horoscopes

In the " changing pattern of marriage", it was observed that in majority of the families studied the practice of matching horoscopes of the spouses is prevalent. There we had not cross tabulated the extent of prevalence of this practice with the forms of families, simply because of our impression that this practice is not prevalent among all the castes. Here we may pick up the uncovered dimension. Table 8.5(a) shows that custom of matching horoscopes of the spouses is very much determined by the caste background of the families.

Table 8.5(a) : Caste, family type and the practice of matching horoscopes

Caste	*Percentages of families where the practice is not prevalent*	
	Nuclear	*Joint*
Upper	5.2	4.3
Lower	42.1	21.6

Table 8.5(a) also shows that matching of horoscopes is more strictly adhered to in the upper caste families than the lower caste families. In this regard, therefore, the upper caste families are more traditional than lower caste families. The cross-tabulation of the extent of prevalence of this practice with the economic status of the families does not show any significant importance of this variable. Class seems to be in no way significantly related with the prevalence of this custom. To support our contention we present Table 8.5(b) containing the cross

tabulation of economic status of different types of families and the extent of prevalence of this practice.

Table 8.5(b) : Economic status, family type and practice of matching horoscopes

Income groups	Percentage of the families where this practice is not prevalent	
	Nuclear	*Joint*
1. Families having monthly income of Rs. 300 or below	34.7	0
2. Families having monthly income between Rs. 300 and 800	2.5	55.5
3. Families having monthly income of Rs. 801 or above	28.5	7.6

Arranged Marriage versus Love Match

Earlier we have noticed that a majority of respondents from all types of families prefer arranged marriage, and love match has yet to gain ground. Here on the basis of an analysis of the caste and class characteristics of respondents preferring love marriage to arranged marriage, we find that the caste of respondents is an important variable affecting their attitude towards love match [See Table 8.6(a)].

Table 8.6 (a) : Caste, family type and preference for love match over arranged marriage

Caste	*Percentage of respondents preferring love match*	
	Nuclear	*Joint*
Upper	22.8	13.0
Lower	17.5	04.3

Table 8.6(a) shows that upper caste respondents are more modern than lower caste respondents so far as the preference for love match is concerned. Here the upper castes seem to be in a larger percentage oriented towards new trends than the lower castes. However, a cross

tabulation of the extent of preference for love match and economic status of the families of the respondents shows that in case of nuclear families there is a progressive correlation between economic status of families and extent of preference for love marriage [See Table 8.6 (b)]. This, however, does not appear to be the position in case of joint families. This indicates that economic status of the families in determining the family's preference for love match has limited influence.

Table 8.6(b) : Economic status, family type and preference for love match

Income groups	*Percentage of respondents preferring love match*	
	Nuclear	*Joint*
1. Families having monthly income of Rs. 300 or below	10.1	0
2. Families having monthly income between Rs. 301 and 800	34.2	44.4
3. Families having monthly income of Rs. 800 or above	42.8	0

Participation of Bridegroom in the Selection of Bride

If we analyse the caste and economic status of the families where bridegrooms are allowed full participation in the selection of bride, we find that, so far the caste of such respondents is concerned, in case of nuclear family the upper castes are more liberal in allowing full participation to the bridegroom in selection of his bride [See Table 8.7(a)]. The position becomes quite contrary in case of the joint families.

Table 8.7 (a) : Caste and the type of families where the bridegrooms fully participate in the selection of bride.

Caste	*Percentage of families where full participation is allowed*	
	Nuclear	*Joint*
Upper	33.3	17.3
Lower	22.8	26.0

Caste does not appear to affect both types of families in the same direction. The economic status of such families also does not reveal any positive correlation with the participation of bridegrooms in the selection of brides [See Table 8.7(b)].

Table 8.7 (b) : Economic status and the type of the families where the bridegroom fully participates in the selection of bride

Income group	*Percentage of families allowing full participation*	
	Nuclear	*Joint*
1. Families having monthly income of Rs. 300 or below	30.4	14.2
2. Families having monthly income between Rs. 301 and 800	18.4	55.5
3. Families having monthly income of Rs. 801 or above	42.8	23.0

Attitude towards Co-education

If we delineate the caste and economic status of the families favouring co-education as a system of education, we find that caste is an important factor determining the attitudes of respondents of both joint and nuclear families. Table 8.8(a) shows that upper caste persons are more in favour of co-education than lower caste persons. This holds good for both types of the family. In the same way economic status of the respondent's families appear to be significantly related to their attitude with regard to co-education. Table 8.8(b) shows that there is a positive correlation between the economic status and acceptance of co-education as a system of education.

Table 8.8 (a) : Caste, family type and acceptance of co-education

Caste	*Percentage of respondent accepting co-education as system of education*	
	Nuclear	*Joint*
Upper	57.8	69.5
Lower	43.8	30.4

With the rise in income, the attitudes of respondents also become more and more oriented towards modernity. Conversely it can be held that lower the income of the respondents, the greater will be his conservativeness. This is natural and can be explained by the fact that since in the Hindu society a girl is considered somebody else's property, a respondent from an economically depressed family may not invest anything from his limited resources to educate the girl. Instead he will save something to be spent for her marriage. But as income increases, the economic bottlenecks are removed and then he might afford this luxury of educating the girl unless he is highly traditional.

Table 8.8 (b) : Economic status, family type and acceptance of co-education

Income group	*Percentage of respondents accepting co-education as a system of education*	
	Nuclear	*Joint*
1. Families having monthly income of Rs. 300 or below	40.5	21.4
2. Families having monthly income between Rs. 301 and 800	63.1	47.3
3. Families having monthly income of Rs. 801 and above	85.7	84.6

It may be pointed out that both caste and class appear to have distinct areas of influence in the affairs of the family. In determining what type of behavioural pattern is congruent with the family status, both caste and economic status have been observed to be operative, of course, with different intensity. This is, in a way, quite natural. In the past, class, caste and power coincided. "Belonging to one or another caste group was the basis of one's identity in ritual, political and economic realms", (Beteille, 1966). In recent years there has been a dissonance between economic status and caste position. Thus, in a single caste we can find men of diverse social statuses. This is bound to weaken the hold of most pervasive caste system and increased role of the economic status of a family in shaping the interactional pattern, value system operative in the family. But since the impact of a very old system (the caste system) cannot be wiped out quickly, we find that even today caste is an institution of prodigious strength in many spheres of our family life.

To sum up, in this chapter it has been pointed out that in the past, caste, being an all pervasive institution, affected the behavioural pattern of an individual. It was, in fact, the most important factor regulating the status, behaviour and value system of Hindus. Advent of industrialization gave birth to certain groups based on economic accomplishments. It is said that the emergence of these classes is inimical to the very existence of the caste system. In order to see to what extent class has weakened the hold of caste system we have taken eight aspects of family life and tried to cross tabulate the responses with the caste background of the families and their class belongingness separately. The analysis has revealed that there are certain areas of family life where, between caste and class, class is important, while in others, caste is dominant. There are areas in which the two are simultaneously operative. To elaborate, we can say that in deviation from role conventionality in handling of money, preference for deferred gratification, role of woman in decision-making concerning selection of bride are spheres where the strong impact of economic status of the family is quite clearly visible and where caste seems to be losing ground, but in horoscope matching and preference for love marriage, the influence of caste is clearly strong and here class position does not cast its influence. These are the regions in which either of the two systems of social stratification is important. However, there are certain items where both caste and class are very effective. These are the areas of husband-wife relationship and acceptance of co-education. In the area of decision-making with regard to selection of bride the economic status of the family affects the pattern, at least in the case of nuclear family.

In brief, we can say that urbanization and modernization appear to run against the gamut of caste and the traditional patterns governed by caste and crumbling under the influence of modern secular trends, yet wiping out caste is not so easy to be achieved so soon. In other words, although class as variable has penetrated into the fabric of social relationship to affect the behavioural pattern, yet the importance of caste has not been completely stamped out. The present phase, therefore, appears to be one of transition where the two forces are competing against each other.

9

EDUCATION AND THE FAMILY

"IT IS well recognized that the outlook and methods of education prevalent in a society have a far-reaching significance and influence upon the other social institutions of that society" (Prabhu, 1954: 102). In fact, among the four parts of the larger society "closely related to education, the family occupies an important position" (Gore and Chitnis, 1967). Particularly "in an expanding industrial society one cannot be fully understood without the other" (Ross, 1961: 234). In a simple primitive society, it is the family which is responsible for inculcating of adult occupational roles. But with the advent of industrialization, formal education has emerged as an equally potent agency for socializing an individual particularly in inculcation of modern occupational roles. Now in a majority of cases the kinship system is no longer a channel for inculcating modern occupational roles from one generation to another. Now formal education provides an individual with a firm anchor for selecting occupational roles in modern society. This point of contract between education and the family system has a number of implications for each other and though both have "different types of interest and have different value emphases, they both mutually influence each other" (Gore and Desai, 1967:6). " The search and taking of modern career positions suiting the educational accomplishments of the individual often compel him to leave his ancestral joint family implying weaker ties with the joint family. It is also said that, by emphasizing the individual, the formal education put before the people the concept of the type of family contrary to the prevailing concept of joint family" (Desai, 1964). To the extent that the effect of education demands re-definition of the roles of wife and mother, husband and son, it "seems to have a far-reaching influence on the institution of marriage, the dowry system, authority in the home, joint family obligations, the position of the aged and child rearing practice" (Gore and

Chitnis, *op. cit.*, 340). While education influences family, the family type also by reinforcing its ways of thinking through language patterns, habits, mode of living, ritual interaction patterns, ceremonies, has both conservative as well as supportive effects on education. The ability or inability of parents to guide their children, financial status of the family, patterns of freedom and authority in the family affect education to a considerable extent.

In this chapter, we propose to study the inter-relation of education and the family. This will include, firstly, the attitudinal dimensions of respondents of different family types and of different educational accomplishments in each family type towards certain recent trends in education and with regard to educational aspirations for children, in order to see the relationship between (i) the family type on the one hand and acceptance of new trends in education and educational aspirations for children on the other, and (ii) the educational attainments of respondents in each family type, on the one hand, and acceptance of new trends in education and educational aspiration for children, on the other. Secondly, this would involve an attempt to analyse the role of educational achievement of the head of the family to alter his attitudinal dimensions as well as the behavioural pattern of the family.

We first take up the study of the attitudes of respondents towards certain issues related with the education of girls. It is said that "the education of girl has a more lasting impact on society than that of a boy. When the educated girl becomes a mother and the mistress of a household, she will see to it that her children receive education even though it may mean some sacrifice and inconvenience for the family" (Sachchidananda, 1967: 216). "A complex interaction operates between education of women and marriage, family relationships, the social roles and values, the relationship between men and women, etc." (Phadke, 1967: 197).

The traditional Hindu society is characterised by complete denial of educational opportunities to women. It placed a high premium on pre-pubertal marriage. But, with the opening of vistas of education for women and due to the need of assimilating women with the changing contours of the social life of the technological era, several new problems seeking adjustment have surfaced. One point of choice for the family in this connection is the alternative between the education of a girl and her marriage. An analysis of the replies of the respondents towards a question seeking to specify their choice in the event of such a predicament reveals that in the case of joint family the majority of respondents is of the opinion that in case they have to make a choice between the marriage of the girl and continuance of her education, they would opt for the former. In case of nuclear family the percentage of persons favouring continuance of girl's education and suspension of marriage is lesser. This is natural, since the postponement of marriage for the continuance of education might be inimical to the joint family living because there might be some difficulty in assimilating mature and highly educated women into the kinship group and value system of joint family. But with the rise in the cost of living and not being a haven of social security like the joint family it is in the interest of nuclear family to educate the females as a safety valve to be used in hard times, hence a larger percentage favours the postponement of marriage (Table 9. 1).

As a respondent from a nuclear family said:

> "When I was a student, my father was jobless and my elder brothers did not help me in any way. Now I am earning, but financially I am so tight that I cannot save anything. However, if anything untoward happens to me, the only consolation, I have, is that my wife is a graduate, and her education would be a great source for livelihood, if I am no more".

With the availability of formal education for girls another point of choice is: whether the education of girls should be a preparation for career or preparation for marriage. Table 9. 1 shows that the majority of the respondents of both nuclear and joint families feels that education of girl in their family is education of marriage. This needs to be explained. In India, the role of woman is primarily that of a housekeeper, wife and mother and not or a bread-winner. The inculcation of the roles concerning home-making responsibilities and securing a suitable match for the daughter is the primary duty of a Hindu family. The social norms do not favour parents acceptance of anything in cash or kind from a married daughter. However, the fact that joint family respondents are slightly more conservative than those in nuclear family is an index of a change in the attitudes among nuclear family respondents which are supposed to be more prone to accept modernity than respondents of the joint family.

Among the various innovations in the field of education introduced during 20th century, the phenomenon of co-education is highly significant. The shortage of woman teachers in girls schools often leaves the parents to choose between accepting co-education or defer girl's education. The strict segregation of women from men in many aspects of social life particularly in large joint families may be hypothesized to create negative attitude towards co-education among head of such families. However, the existence of practically no variation in the attitudes of nuclear and joint families goes to corroborate that the family itself is not significant variable to affect respondents attitudes towards co-education.

One more facet of the problem of girl's education is whether they should be allowed to leave parents to pursue their study in some other town. As an expert in home-making and child-rearing, the socialization of girls is primarily done by the family. Allowing a girl to live in hostels marks a step towards modernization. Table 9. 1 presents a picture that social pressures are still strongly against allowing a girl to leave her residence for education. Difficulty of financing their education, the need for their services at home, absence of adequate control in hostels make it foolhardy on the part of parents to provide girls with such latitude. The disasters following such permissiveness are likely to be injurious equally for joint and nuclear families. However, the presence of negative attitudes in somewhat lesser degree in case of nuclear family indicates that nuclear family is more inclined to modernity in education than joint family.

Table 9.1 : Family type and attitude towards girls' education

	Statements	*Percentage saying 'Yes'*	
		Nuclear family	*Joint family*
1.	In the case of a choice between the marriage of a girl and continuance of her education one should allow her to continue her studies	46. 0	26. 0
2.	A girl should be permitted to leave her parents to live in some other town for study	36. 8	26. 0
3.	Co-education as a system of education is favourable	52. 6	52. 1
4.	The education of a girl in my family is for enabling her to take a job in future	11. 7	12. 9

Table 9.1 reveals that, in acceptance of certain new trends in girl's education, the family type is an important variable. Particularly in deferring marriage for education, permitting a girl to live away from the parents and viewing education as preparation for career, the nuclear family is more permissive than the joint family. But so far as acceptance of co-education, as a system of education is concerned, we find that it is not much averse to traditional thinking represented by joint family.

The analysis of the concepts of optimum employment for boys and girls as prevalent among the heads of the different types of family shows that so far as the head's aspiration for male child is concerned, majority of the respondents in both types of family is in favour of imparting highest possible education to them. But the percentage of those specifying post-graduate or above as the level of aspiration for the male child is slightly larger in the case of nuclear family than joint family. This enables us to postulate that the corporate finances of a larger joint family themselves may not be supportive to the extent of boosting the educational aspirations for the boys of joint family. In conformity with the pattern of joint family youngmen might be compelled to cut short their education in order to share family responsibilities. This attitude of the joint family is apparent in the following statement of a member of one of the joint families:

> "After completing my B.A. degree, I wanted to qualify for law and prepare for competitive examinations. But my father insisted that I should share the responsibility of education the younger children, to meet the expenses on my wife and children. Ultimately I had to learn typing and now I am a typist".

Table 9. 2 : Level of aspiration and family type

Level of Aspiration	*Nuclear family*		*Joint family*	
	For Boys Per cent	*For Girls Per cent*	*For Boys Per cent*	*For Girls Per cent*
1. Below Matriculation	7.0	51.7	2.21	45.6
2. Up to B.A.	1.8	16.7	17.4	15.2
3. Professional Degree	6.1	8.8	6.5	10.9
4. M.A. and above	85.1	22.8	83.9	28.3

As regards educational ambition for girls is concerned the role of family type does not appear to be very significant (Table 9. 2).

This is perhaps due to the fact that in no case the parents allow the postponement of the marriage of the girl after a particular age. Higher education will mean delay in marriage of the girl. Higher education for girls would mean payment of higher dowry for marriage, because she will have to be married to a more qualified groom. As a respondent told me:

> "I cannot permit my daughters to continue education beyond matriculation. For a graduate daughter, I will have to search a well placed and better qualified son-in-law. This will need thousands of rupees as dowry".

Till now we examined as to how far the family type is supportive or opposed to education. Now, we shall examine the extent to which education affects the attitudes of respondents of different types of family. Classifying the respondents of each of educational categories as acceptors or rejecters of modernity in education and comparing the

Table 9.3 : Attitude towards family education type and respondents' education

Statements	*Percentage of respondents saying 'yes'*			
	Up to matriculation		*Above matriculation*	
	Nuclear	*Joint*	*Nuclear*	*Joint*
1. In the case of a choice between the marriage of a girl and continuance of her education one should allow her to continue her studies	19. 3	24. 1	56. 6	41. 2
2. A girl should be permitted to leave her parents to live in some other town for higher studies	42. 2	13. 8	50. 9	41. 2
3. Co-education as a system of education is favoured	40. 4	37. 6	64. 9	64. 9
4. The education of a girl in family is for enabling her to take a job in future	4. 3	20. 1	13. 1	6. 25

percentages of acceptors from each educational category in the joint and nuclear families, we find that in both the types of family higher education may be positively correlated with modernization and innovation in the field of education. It shows that those who have some post-high school education are the major acceptors of new arrangements in the field of education (Table 9. 3). This is but natural in the sense that those with higher education reorient their outlook on formal education by adjusting themselves to new environment. They are capable of looking beyond the constructive spheres of tradition and identify themselves with choices of new situations. A smaller percentage of persons from the category, consisting of illiterates or educated upto matriculation, shows that their marriage in the traditional norms of the society is deeper as compared to the category of persons having post-matriculation education, and the former are not prepared to move out of it.

If we cross-tabulate the educational aspirations for males and females of the family of different types with the educational qualification of the heads, so far the educational aspirations for boys are concerned, education seems to be a significant variable in nuclear family, more qualified men setting high educational aspirations (Table 9. 4). In joint family the picture is slightly different. A comparison of the aspirations for respondents of the two educational categories reveals that less educated persons have higher aspirations in some more cases than the high educated persons. But here, too, the respondent mentioning lowest aspiration belongs to the category of less educated.

Table 9.4 : Family, type, education of respondents and levels of aspirations for males

	Levels of aspirations	*Nuclear family*		*Joint family*	
		Upto Matric Per cent	*Above Matric Per cent*	*Upto Matric Per cent*	*Above Matric Per cent*
1.	Matriculation or below	14. 0	0	3. 4	0
2.	B.A.	3. 5	0	17. 2	17. 6
3.	Professional	28. 1	38. 6	24. 1	29. 4
4.	M.A. and above	54. 4	61. 4	58. 3	53. 0

So far as the educational aspirations of women are concerned, education is very significant in case of nuclear family. Better educated persons have higher educational aspiration for girls as compared to less educated persons (Table 9. 5). In the case of the joint family, education does not seem to be so significant, as a larger percentage of both less educated and more educated respondents does not want to send girls to colleges. But here also we find that among the persons who prescribed highest ambitions for girls, the percentage of better educated is higher when compared to less educated. Thus, the setting of educational ambition by respondents of different educational accomplishments in both types of family shows that education seems to be positively related with high education aspirations of men and women of nuclear family. In case of joint family, it is not so significantly related, the difference in many cases being very narrow.

Table 9.5 : Family type, education of respondents and levels of aspirations for females

	Levels of aspirations	*Nuclear family*		*Joint Family*	
		Upto Matric Per cent	*Above Matric Per cent*	*Upto Matric Per cent*	*Above Matric Per cent*
1.	Matriculation or below	73. 7	29. 8	44. 9	47. 1
2.	B.A.	8. 8	24. 6	17. 2	17. 6
3.	Professional	5. 3	12. 3	13. 8	5. 9
4.	M.A. and above	12. 2	33. 3	24. 1	29. 4

Lastly, we proceed to the analysis of education of the head of the family as an independent variable determining the attitudinal dimensions of the respondents and behavioural pattern in the family with regard to certain other facets of family life. If we take up the various dimensions of family in the light of which we examined the importance of caste and economic position of family as independent variables, altering the responses of different families, we get a number of interesting findings. In the first place there appears to be certain facets of family life where positive correlation between high education and modernity exists. From Table 9. 6 it is quite clear that in both types of the family highly educated persons appear to be more prone to deferred gratification than the less educated persons. In their preference for a love-match over arranged marriages, highly educated respondents appear to be more liberal than the less educated respondents. Joint families with highly educated respondents are more equalitarian in husband-wife interaction than the families with less educated respondents.

Table 9.6 : Education of the head and the attitudinal dimensions of the respondents and behavioural pattern in different types of the family

	Dimensions	*Nuclear family*		*Joint family*	
		Above Matric Per cent	*Up to Matric Per cent*	*Above Matric Per cent*	*Up to Matric Per cent*
1.	Exception from role conventionality in handling of money	15. 7	21. 0	17. 6	17. 2
2.	Restrictions to free talk between husband and wife	–	–	17. 6	31. 0
3.	Woman as the most effective decision-maker (in choice of bride)	10. 5	17. 5	41. 1	17. 2
4.	Orientation to deferred gratification as reflected in preference for continuation of study to taking up a job	87. 8	56. 2	53. 0	51. 8
5.	Non-prevalence of the practice of matching horoscopes of spouses before marriage	1. 7	45. 6	5. 8	17. 2
6.	Complete freedom to boys in selection of bride	31. 5	26. 3	17. 6	10. 3
7.	Preference to love match over arranged marriage	24. 5	15. 7	17. 6	3. 4

Families with highly educated respondents appear to be more permissive in allowing boys complete freedom in the selection of their spouses. However, it is also apparent that in exception to role conventionality and the role of women as the most effective decision-maker, the education of the head is not significantly related. In case of the practice of matching horoscopes also it cannot be postulated that high education is making respondents more and more abandoned old practices. In brief we can say that while the attitudes of the respondents appear to be significantly related with education, it is not the position in case of behavioural pattern characterising the families. It cannot be said that high education of the heads of family is necessarily bound to alter the behavioural pattern of the families in all cases.

To sum up, in this chapter an attempt has been made to study the attitudinal dimensions of the respondents of different family types and of different educational accomplishments towards certain new trends in education and with regard to educational aspirations for children. We have tried to see the impact of the education of the head as an independent variable determining the attitudes of the respondents and behavioural patterns in the families. The analysis revealed that the family type is an important variable in acceptance of certain modern trends in education. The nuclear family appears to be more inclined to accept those trends than the joint family. Corporate finance alone is not sufficient to boost educational aspirations for the boys of joint family. Higher education appears to be positively correlated with acceptance of innovations in education. In other dimensions of the family, education of the head appears to be a strong variable in shaping the attitudes of respondents. But in shaping the internal processes, education is not a strong variable in all the cases.

10

SUMMARY AND CONCLUSIONS

THROUGH this work we have made a modest attempt to add to the available data on the Indian family. The work was conducted in a region which, more or less, has remained a *terra incognita* in the research on family. So the data collected for this study will prove data from a region which, in turn, will help sociologists to locate common and unique features of the Indian family in different geo-ethnic and social environments

The study was conducted in Patna, the capital of Bihar. In all we studied 160 Hindu families residing in this cultural and administrative centre. Since the structural basis of Hinduism is the caste system, we tried to cover families of various castes. Among the numerically dominant castes residing in Patna, we selected eight castes. Each caste-group constituted a cell and from each cell twenty respondents were selected. In order to further widen the scope of the study, attempts were made to incorporate families belonging to different income brackets. Interview and observation were used as the basic tools for collection of data for the present study. In the initial stage of the study a semi-structured schedule was pre-tested to make the interview schedule a structured one. We went beyond the fixed questions to delve deep into the phenomenon studies. The broad dimensions covered in the study are: compositional forms and types of the family, pattern of inter-personal relationship, distribution of power, pattern of role-allocation, patterns of marriage, all as operative in the families, and the inter-relations between family and education and family and occupation. These were taken as dependent variables. The most important independent variable has been the family type. Besides this, education, income and caste have also been treated as independent variables with regard to certain dimensions. With this background, we studied the behavioural pattern of the family and attitudinal dimensions of the respondents in a social environment brought into force as a result of urbanization.

A careful reading of the results and discussions as contained in the preceding pages reveals a number of significant results.

To start with the compositional structure of the family, the majority of the families covered in this study were the nuclear type consisting of husband, wife, unmarried children with or without one or more additional kin. The presence of the additional kin in many of the nuclear families is indicative of the fact that structurally nuclear families of our study are quite distinct from the strictly nuclear families of highly industrialized societies. The existence of a number of joint families, on the other hand, indicates that the growth of urbanization has not been too strong to stop the growth of joint families. Proceeding further, the ordering of relationship in the case of joint families was lineal in majority of the cases. Through the analysis of the internal processes in the family, the pattern of interaction in day-to-day life was regulated by age, sex and relationship roles. Even than father-child relationship was largely equalitarian. Majority of the fathers-in-law were maintaining relations of avoidance with their daughters-in-law. On the other hand, the sibling relationship was not characterized by the bond of affection in majority of the cases. The position of women might not servile, but it was clear that the norm deterring a couple to go out together to some place is not a social fiction. Social forces were found to be operative in prohibiting one to go with his wife in certain families. But in majority of the cases this tradition was devalued. Geographically separated nuclear families of sons or parents helped each other in time of crisis. Therefore, while the geographical mobility necessitated by urbanization might compel sons and parents to live separately, the separated nuclear units were found to be enmeshed in an innate network of mutual aid and social relations.

The analysis of the internal division of labour within family on the basis of activities selected from the behavioural field of the family revealed that the performance of strenuous economic activities was the domain of men, while the regions of child-care and household duties were in most cases the main provinces of women. Analysing the extent of exception in the conventional pattern of task performance, it became clear that the degree of deviation was greater in regions which are domains of men. Thus, the fear of being unconventional and existence of social censure against participation in women's work was found to be strong in the case of men doing women's work. Next, we analysed the internal process of family to depict the power structure in the family. Here we found that in majority of cases eldest male was perceived as the final authority. This is in conformity with traditional normative extrapolations. Moreover, the pattern of decision-making was found to be less syncratic in majority of cases. After the eldest men, the eldest women was found to be the next powerful locus of power. But generally speaking, women were found to be low-powered than men. This confirms that men's dominance in each family affair is too deeply set to show any radical change due to an outside stimulus.

The analysis of the pattern of marriage revealed that during the last forty years the age of marriage of boys or girls was rising. In recent years, difficulty in securing jobs, long spell of education and occupation preparation are bound to raise the age of marriage. Adult marriage gives birth to a desire for freedom of choice of the spouses in the hearts of boys as well as girls. Consequently, families were permitting more and more participation in the selection of life partners to men. Strict mores were found to be operative in favour of maintaining age difference between husband and wife. Opinions were largely in favour of endogamous marriages, the practice of matching horoscopes, etc. This postulates that these traditions are deeply set in the Hindu culture. Majority of the respondents were found to be preferring the old way so far as the above traditions are concerned. Laws have been enacted to permit divorce. Secular environment of urbanization permits inter-caste marriage. In fact, all these are index of changing attitudes and values. But, so far as the prevalence of inter-caste marriage and divorce is concerned, legislative measures and new socio-psychological environment have not been found to be conducive enough to witness any radical change in these spheres. The social status of the family, education of the spouse, economic position and physical attractiveness were found to be important factors in selection of spouses.

Analysing the inter-relations between family and occupation we observed that families in general were highly impatient towards the educated unemployed. Certain occupations were still found to be labelled as derogatory. Women, wherever, employed, were only secondary bread-earners.

As mentioned earlier, the most important independent variable of the study has been the family composition, now here we present in brief the differences in the attitudinal propensity and behavioural patterns of the nuclear and joint families. The relationship between family type and responses concerning various dimensions of the family highlighted the fact that while in most cases the joint families responses were very much in conformity with traditionally prescribed norms, values or behavioural patterns responses of the nuclear families reflected traits of progress and modernity in greater extent than the joint family. The joint family was more adhering to the traditional limited relations between father-in-law and daughter-in-law. It was a greater deterrent against participation by men in duties which were the domains of women. In decision-making joint family was found to be more autocratic than nuclear family. With regard to all recent trends in marriage, for example permissiveness to inter-caste marriage, love-match, participation in selection of bridegroom, practice of seeing girl before marriage, divorce, etc., the joint family appeared to be less accommodative than nuclear family. Almost similar type of conservativeness and traditionality was also revealed in the acceptance of new trends in education. Apart from this, in certain other dimensions joint family appeared to have responded greatly to change in the socio-psychological environment generated by the forces of urbanization. For example, in father-child relationship and allowing younger couples to go out together, joint family was found to be characterized by greater equalitarianism than nuclear family. In allowing the couples to meet freely, joint family was again found to be highly accommodative. Again the joint family as a haven of security appeared to be more sympathetic to the educated unemployed than the nuclear family. Nonetheless, it was also found to be more prone to immediate gratification and to accept low status jobs than the nuclear family. These might be due to the economic compulsions.

As mentioned earlier, apart from the composition of families, the caste and the economic position of the family were also used as independent variables. The correlation of the various dimensions of the family with the caste and class background of respondents revealed in the first place that caste was not at all unimportant factor in altering the structure of family types. The joint family did not appear to be a preserve of upper caste people, yet the nuclear families of the upper castes were found to be structurally more supplemented than those of the lower castes. Thus they possessed the rudiments of jointness in greater degree than the lower caste families. The analysis further revealed the existence of positive correlation between income of the family and jointness. Apart from these, the strength of caste and class as independent variables was also examined with reference to eight issues taken from different family dimensions. It was found that in deviation from role conventionality in handling of money, proneness to deferred gratification, women's position in decision-making with regard to selection of brides were the regions where caste was found to be losing ground. In these regions the economic status of the family was found to be significantly related. But we cannot say that caste has lost all its importance in shaping family life. For example, in sphere of marriage, caste was found to be a strong factor. Besides, caste and class both were found to be effectively operative in the area of husband-wife relationship and permissiveness to co-education.

Likewise, we also treated education of the head of family as one of the independent variables. In the first place we found that positive correlation existed between nuclear family and high education. High education and acceptance to new trends in education were also found to be positively related. In the case of level of aspiration for one's children's education, education of respondents was found to be more effectively related in nuclear family than joint family. Correlation of education of the head with certain other dimensions of family revealed that in their attitudinal propensity highly educated persons were found to be more oriented to deferred gratification. They favoured love-match to arranged marriage in greater degree than the low educated respondents. Again, in families with high educated heads complete freedom in selection of bride was found to be available to larger number of persons than the families with less educated heads. Families with high educated heads showed less exception from role-conventionality in handling of money than the families with low-educated heads. Horoscope was found to be prevalent more in families with high educated heads than families with less educated heads. In the joint families with low educated heads more restrictions in husband-wife interaction prevailed than the families with highly educated heads.

The findings of the present work thus corroborates the hypothesis that in the event of urban forces impinging upon family life, the nuclear family will be more prone to the forces of change than joint family. The second hypothesis that, in the urban setting, class would replace caste as the dominant variable does not get full support. Though class has penetrated into the fabric of social life, yet caste has not entirely faded out as an influencing force. The correlation of education with dimensions of family life corroborated the third hypothesis that families with highly educated heads would reveal patterns proximating to modernity.

In brief, we can say, first, that on basis of this sample survey although one cannot make very specific statements to cover the whole of the Hindu society, we can spell out some of the dominant trends in the direction of family change.

If the theoretical extrapolations depicting traditional family patterns are taken as reference points to locate the changes, we can say that the previous social profiles of family structure have greatly changed. However, the changes taking place are not witnessed in all spheres of the family. Nor are changes uniform for the various facets of family life. All dimensions of the society are not witnessing change in the same manner. Some spheres have been radically affected by the process of change while others are lagging behind. In other words, although, under the influence of urbanization and secularization, traditional societies are crumbling down, yet there are spheres where traditions still has a stronghold on the people. On the whole, the Hindu society in general and the Hindu family in particular at the present time appear to be curious mixture of traditionalism and modernity.

Analysis of the behavioural pattern and attitudinal dimension of the nuclear and joint families reveals that in value-orientations behavioural pattern, the family type appears to be an important variable. The nuclear and joint families differ with each other in a number of cases. True, both the nuclear and joint families have been affected by the process of change and changes have penetrated all types of family systems causing necessary adjustments in their behaviour. The comparison of the responses of the nuclear and joint families reflects a contrast between more progressive and secular families on the one hand and tradition-oriented families on the other. The nuclear families were found to be more exposed to individualism and modernity than the joint family. The pattern and degree of change in the two units differ in the different spheres of family life. However, though the family is nuclear in some cases, it is not completely isolated. Geographical distance does not mean interactional isolation. Therefore, it cannot be said that "the effect of industrialization and urbanization upon the family system of the newly developing areas of the East are going to be a mere repetition of the past Western" (Dasgupta, 1965 : 287-88). The Hindu nuclear families even when structurally isolated revealed behavioural pattern, appropriate more to familial norms than to bureaucratic norms. The degree of economic status and traditionalism of the caste system are also important variables of family change. Both have their own areas of influences. Economic factor has penetrated into the fabric of social relationship, yet the importance of caste is not altogether stamped out. In the present phase the two are competing against each other.

Education by inculcating secular values and modern traits in individuals is inimical to familial norms and tradition. The majority of the people with education and secular orientation is moving in some degree against tradition.

At the end we append a tabulated brief summary where extent of variations, caused due to various independent variables, are shown. Following Gore (1968) we have also used four categories to indicate measure of variation. These are :

Small or negligible – A variation of less than eight per cent.
Moderate – A variation of eight per cent to 14 per cent.
Large – A variation of above 14 per cent to 29 per cent.
Very large – A variation of above 29 per cent.

Division of Labour in the Family

	Dimensions	*Independent Variable(s)*	*Variation, if any*	*Extent of variation*	*Reference Table*
1.	Handling of money	Family type	Joint family less strict in observance of role conventionality than the nuclear family	Small	3.1
		Caste and family type	No consistent variation	–	8.1(a)
		Class and family type	High income groups more susceptible to deviation in role conventionality in both family types	Small to large	8.1(b)
		Education of the head	No consistent variation	–	9.6
2.	Purchase of vegetables	Family type	Nuclear family more prone to deviate from role conventionality	Small	3.1
3.	Purchase of clothes for children	Family type	Nuclear family more prone to deviate from role-conventionality	Small	3.1
4.	Bathing of the children	Family type	Nuclear family more prone to deviate from role conventionality	Moderate	3.2
5.	Feeding the children	Family type	Nuclear family more prone to deviate from role conventionality	Moderate	3.2
6.	Telling stories to children	Family type	Joint family more prone to deviate from role conventionality	Moderate	3.2
7.	Teaching children at home	Family type	Nuclear family more prone to deviate from role conventionality	Large	3.2

Inter-personal Relationship in the Family

	Dimensions	Independent	Variation, if any	Extent of variation	Reference Table
1.	Permissiveness to couples to go out together	Family type	Nuclear family more permissive than joint family	Small and large	4.1
2.	Egalitarianism in father-children relationship	Family type	Nuclear family more egalitarian than joint family	Small	–
3.	Avoidance between father-in-law and daughter-in-law	Family type	Nuclear family less strict than the joint family	Moderate	4.2
4.	Permissiveness to spouses to talk freely to each other in the joint family	Caste family type	Upper caste less rigid than lower caste in both types of family	Large	8.2(a)
		Class family type	No consistant variation	–	8.2(b)
		Education of the head	More freedom in the families with highly educated heads	Moderate	9.6
5.	Fear and respect to elder siblings	Family type	Nuclear family more strict than joint family	Moderate	4.3

Power and Authority in the Family

	Dimensions	*Independent Variable(s)*	*Variation, if any*	*Extent of variation*	*Reference Table*
1.	The perception of oldest male as the final decision-maker with regard to				
	(a) Schooling of chilren	Family type	Nuclear family perceives eldest male as the final decision maker in more cases than the joint family	Large	5.1 (a)
	(b) Selection of bride-grooms	Family type	Nuclear family perceives eldest male as the final decision maker in more cases than the joint family	Moderate	5.1(a)
	(c) Selection of brides	Family type	Nuclear family perceives eldest male as the final decision maker in more cases than joint family	Moderate	5.2(a)
	(d) Permission of women going home to their parents	Family type	Nuclear family perceives eldest male as the final decision maker in more cases than joint family	Very large	5.1(a)
	(e) Bringing in relatives	Family type	Nuclear family perceives eldest male as the final decision-maker in more cases than joint family	Moderate	5.1(b)

(Contd.)

	Dimensions	*Independent Variable(s)*	*Variation if any*	*Extent of variation*	*Reference Table*
2.	Pattern of decision-making with regard to				
	(a) Schooling	Family type	Nuclear family more autocratic than joint family	Small	5.2
	(b) Selection of bride	Family type	Joint family more autocratic than nuclear family	Large	5.2
	(c) Selection of bride-grooms	Family type	Joint family more autocratic than nuclear family	Moderate	5.2
	(d) Permission of women going home to their parents	Family type	Joint family more autocratic than nuclear family	Moderate	5.2
	(e) Bringing in relatives	Family type	Joint family more autocratic than nuclear family	Large	5.2

Work and Family

	Dimensions	Independent Variable(s)	Variation, if any	Extent of variation	Reference Table
1.	Patience and sympathy towards educated unemployed	Family type	Joint family shows greater patience than the nuclear family	Small	6.1
2.	Preference of job to education	Family type	Joint family more prone to immediate gratification	Large	6.2
		Caste and family type	No consistent variation	–	8.4(a)
		Class and family type	Lower the income greater the orientation towards immediate gratification in both types of family	Large	8.4(b)
		Education of the head and the family type	Higher education and deferred gratification positively related in both types of the family	Very large–nuclear family Small-joint family	9.6
3.	Perception of manual work or job or a peon	Family type	Joint family less traditional	Moderate	6.3

Pattern of Marriage

Dimensions	*Independent Variable(s)*	*Variation, if any*	*Extent of variation*	*Reference Table*
1. Encouragement to inter-caste marriage				
(a) When a boy of the family of party to hypergamous marriage	Family type	Joint family more conservative than the nuclear family	Small	7.5
(b) When a girl of the family is a party to hypergamous marriage	Family type	Joint family more conservative than the nuclear family	Small	7.5
(c) When a boy of the family is a party to hypogamous marriage	Family type	Joint family more conservative than the nuclear family	–	7.5
(d) When a girl of the family is a party to hypogamous marriage	Family type	Nuclear family more conservative than the joint family	Small	7.5
2. Love match vs arranged marriage	Family type	Nuclear family prefers love match in longer cases than the joint family	Moderate	7.6
	Family type	Upper caste persons more in favour of love match in both types of family	Small–nuclear family Moderate–joint family	8.6(a)
	Class and family type	No consistent variation	–	8.6(b)

(Contd.)

Dimensions	*Independent Variable(s)*	*Variation, if any*	*Extent of variation*	*Reference Table*
	Education of the head and family type	Higher the education greater the preference for love match in both types of family	Moderate	9.6
3. Participation of a man in the selection of his bride	Family type	Joint family more rigid	Moderate	9.6
	Caste and family type	No consistent variation	Moderate	7.7(a)
	Class and family type	No consistent variation	–	8.7(b)
	Education of the head and family type	Higher education or higher latitude positively related in both types of family	Moderate	9.6
4. Practice of matching horoscope	Family type	Joint family more tradition oriented	Moderate	7.9
	Caste and family type	Upper caste persons more rigid	Nuclear-very large Joint-large	8.5(a)
	Class and family type	No consistent variation	–	8.5(b)
	Education	Less prevalent in less educated	Nuclear–very large Joint–moderate	9.6
5. Importance of certain attributes in the selection of bride				

(Contd.)

Dimensions	*Independent Variable(s)*	*Variation, if any*	*Extent of variation*	*Reference Table*
(a) Social status of the family	Family type	Joint family attaches greater importance	Small	7.10
(b) Education	Family type	Nuclear family attaches greater importance	Small	7.10
(c) Economic status	Family type	Nuclear family attaches greater importance	Moderate	7.10
(d) Attractive-ness	Family type	Nuclear family	Small	7.10
6. Importance of certain attributes in the selection of bride-groom				
(a) Social status of the family	Family type	Nuclear family gives more importance than the joint family	Small	7.10
(b) Education	Family type	Nuclear family gives more importance than the joint family	Small	7.10
(c) Economic status	Family type	Nuclear family gives more importance than the joint family	Small	7.10
(d) Physical attractive-ness	Family type	Nuclear family gives more importance than the joint family	Small	7.10
7. Seeing girl before marriage	Family type	Nuclear family more liberal	Moderate	7.11
8. Permissiveness to divorce	Family type	Nuclear family more liberal	Moderate	7.12

Education and Family

Dimensions	*Independent variable(s)*	*Variation, if any*	*Extent of variations*	*Reference Table*
1. Permissiveness to new trends in education				
(a) Permitting a girl to leave her parents to study in some other town	Family type	Nuclear family more permissive	Moderate	9.1
	Education and the head family type	High education and greater permissiveness positively related in both types	Nuclear–Moderate Joint–large	9.3
(b) Marriage vs education of girls	Family type	Nuclear family favours education of girl to marriage in more cases	Large	9.1
Family type and education of head	High education and more preference for education positively related in both types		Nuclear–very large Joint–large	9.3
(c) Education for girl for job or for marriage	Family type	Nuclear family gives education for marriage in more cases than joint family	Small	9.1
	Education of the head or family type	No consistent variation		9.3

(Contd.)

Dimensions	*Independent Variable(s)*	*Variation, if any*	*Extent of variation*	*Reference Table*
(d) Permissiveness to co-education	Family type	Nuclear family more permissive	Small	9.1
	Caste and family type	No consistent variation	–	8.8(a)
	Class and family type	Higher in one group more permissive in both types	Nuclear–large Joint–large and very large	8.8(b)
	Education of head and family type	High educated persons more permissive	Large	9.3

BIBLIOGRAPHY

Books

Anderson, Nel and Ishwaran, K. (1965) *Urban Sociology*, Asia Publishing House, Bombay.

Anshen, Ruth Nanda, (1949) *The Family : Its Function and Destiny*, Harper and Row Publishers, New York.

Bachmann, Hedvig, (1942) *On the Soul of the Indian Women as Reflected in the Folklore of Konkan*, Tipografic Rangel, Bastora, India Portuguesa.

Barber, R.E., (1939) *Marriage and the Family*, McGraw-Hill, New York.

Berreman, G.D., (1963) *Hindus of Himalayas*, Oxford University Press, Bombay.

Beteille, A., (1966) *Caste, Class and Power: Changing Patterns of Stratification in a Tanjore Village*, Oxford University Press, Bombay.

Bossard, J.H.S., (1953) *Parents and Child*, University of Pennsylvania, Philadelphia.

Bott, Elizabeth, (1957) *Family and Social Network*, Tavistock, London.

Burgess, E.W. and Lock, H.J., (1953) *The Family*, American Book, New York.

Chhibar, Y.P., (1968) *From Caste to Class*, Associated Publishing House, New Delhi.

Christensen, Harold, T. (ed.), (1964) *Handbook of Marriage and Family*, Rand McNally and Co., Chicago.

Cox, O.C., (1959) *Caste, Class and Race*, Monthly Review Press, New York.

Dahl, Robert A., (1963) *Modern Political Analysis*, Prentice Hall Inc., Englewood Cliffs, New Jersey.

Desai, A.R., (1948) *The Social Background of Indian Nationalism*, Oxford University Press, Bombay.

Desai, I.P., (1964) *Some Aspects of Family in Mahuva*, Asia Publishing House, Bombay.

Dore, Ronald, P., (1958) *City Life in Japan*, University of California Press, Berkeley.

Dube, S.C., (1955) *Indian Village*, Routledge and Kegan Paul, London.

———, (1963) 'Men's and Women's Roles in India : A Sociological Review' in *Women in the New Asia*, (ed.) Barbara Ward, United Nations Educational Scientific and Cultural Organization.

Epstein, T.S., (1962) *Economic Development and Social Change in South India*, Manchester University Press, Manchester.

Farber, Bernard, (ed.) (1966) *Kinship and Family Organization*, John Wiley and Sons, Inc. New York.

Fortes, Meyer, (1958) *The Development Cycle in Domestic Group*, Cambridge University Press, Cambridge.

Gangopadhyay, Bela, (1964) *Marriage Regulations Among Certain Castes of Bengal*, Deccan College, Dissertation Series 25, Poona.

Ghurye, G.S., (1952) *Caste and Class in India*, Popular Book Depot, Bombay.

Goode, W.J., (1961) 'Family Disorganization' in *Contemporary Social Problems*, ed. by R.K.Merton and R.A. Nisbet, New York.

———, (1965) *The Family*, Prentice-Hall of India (Pvt.) Ltd., New Delhi.

———, (1967) 'The Family as an Element in the World Revolution' in *In the Study of Society*, ed. by Peter I. Rose, Random House, New York.

———, (1968) *World Revolution and Family Pattern*, The Free Press, New York.

Goode, W.J. and Hatt, P.K., (1952) *Methods in Social Research*, MacGraw-Hill, New York.

Gore, M.S., (1965) 'Traditional Indian Family' in *Comparative Family System*, ed. by M.P. Ninkoff, Haughton and Mifflin, Boston.

———, (1968) *Urbanization and Family Change*, Popular Prakashan, Bombay.

Gore, M.S. and Chitnis, Suma, (1967) 'Sociology and Educational Research' in *Papers in the Sociology of Education in India*, ed. by M.S.Gore, I.P. Desai, Suma Chitnis. National Council of Educational Research and Training, New Delhi.

Gore, M.S. and Desai, I.P., (1967) "The Scope of Sociology of Education", in *Papers in the Sociology of Education in India*, ed. by M.S. Gore, I.P. Desai, Suma Chitnis. National Council of Educational Research and Training, New Delhi.

Gough, E. Iathleen, (1955) 'The Social Structure of a Tanjore Village' in *Village India*, ed. by Mokim Marriot, University of Chicago Press, Chicago.

Harris, C.C., (1969) *The Family*, George Allen and Unwin Ltd., London.

Hate, C.A., (1969) *Changing Status of Women in Post-Independence India*, Allied Publishers Pvt. Ltd., Bombay.

Herbst, P.G., (1961) 'Task Differentiation of Husband and Wife, in Family Activities' in *A Modern Introduction to the Family*, ed. by Norman W. Bell and Ezra F. Vogell, Routledge and Kegan Paul, London.

Hill, Reuben, (1965) 'Decision-making and the Family Life Cycle' in *Social Structure and the Family Generational Relations*, ed. by Ethel Shans and Gardon F. Streib, Prentice Hall Inc., Englewood Cliffs, New Jersey.

Homans, George, C., (1957) *The Human Group*, Routledge and Kegan Paul Ltd., London.

Kanan, C.T., (1963) *Inter-Caste and Inter-Community Marriages in India*, Allied Publishers Pvt. Ltd., Bombay.

Kapadia, K.M., (1959) *Marriage and Family in India*, Oxford University Press, Bombay.

Karve, Irawati, (1953) *Kinship Organization in India*, Deccan College Monograph Series No.11, Deccan College, Poona.

Karve, Irawati, (1963) 'Family Through Six Generations' in *Anthropology on the March*, ed. by Bala Ratnam. The Book Centre and the Social Sciences Association, Madras.

———, (1964) 'Family in India' in *Contemporary India*, ed. by Baidya Nath Verma, Asia Publishing House, Bombay.

Kolenda, Pauline M., (1968) 'Religion, Caste and Family Structure: A Comparative Study of the Indian Joint Family' in *Structure and Change in Indian Society*, ed. by Milton Singer and Bernard, S. Cohn, Aldine Publishing Company, Chicago.

Kuppuswamy, B., (1937) *A Study of Opinion Regarding Marriage and Divorce*, Asia Publishing House, Bombay.

Kurian, George, (1961) *The Indian Family in Transition: A Case Study of Kerala Syrian Christians*, Mouton and Co., Hague.

Lembert, Richard D., (1963) *Workers, Factories and Social Change in India*, Asia Publishing House, Bombay.

Laswell, Harold D. and Kaplan Abraham, (1950) *Power and Society*, Yale University Press, New Haven.

Lazarsfeld, P.F. and Rosenberg, M., (eds.) (1955) *The Language of Social Research: A Reader in the Methodology of the Social Sciences*, The Free Press, New York.

Levy, Dr. Marrion J., (1949) *The Family Revolution in Modern China*, Harvard University Press, Cambridge.

Lewis, Oscar, (1958) *Village Life in Northern India*, University of Illinois Press, Urbana.

Lynch, Owen, M., (1963) 'Some Aspects of Rural-Urban Continuum in India' in *Anthropology on the March*, ed. by Bala Ratnam, The Book Centre, Madras, 1963.

Mace, David and Vora; (1980) *Marriage East and West*. MacGibbon and Kee, London.

Mac Iver, R.N. and Pare, C., (1949) *Society: An Introductory Analysis*, Farrar and Rinehart, New York.

Madan, T.N., (1965) *Family and Kinship: A Study of the Pandits of Rural Kashmir*, Asia Publishing House, Bombay.

Mandelbaum, David G., (1949) 'The Family in India' in *The Family: Its Function and Its Destiny*, ed. by Ruth Nanda Aushen, Harper and Brothers, New York.

Mandelbaum, David G., (1957) *Civilization of India: Changing Dimensions of Indian Society and Culture*, University of Chicago Press, Chicago.

———, (1968) 'Family, Jati and Village' in *Structure and Change in Indian Society*, ed. by Milton Singer and Bernard. S., Cohn, Aldine Publishing Co., Chicago.

Mathur, K.S., (1964) *Caste and Ritual in a Malwa Village*, Asia Publishing House, Bombay.

Mead, Marget, (1963) 'The Impact of Cultural Changes on the Family' in *The Family in the Urban Community*, The Merrilt Palmer School, Deteroit.

Mills, C. Wright, (1963) *Power, Politics and People*, ed. by Irving Louis Horowitz, Oxford University Press, New York.

Murdock, George P., (1949) *Social Structure*, Macmillan, New York.

Norbeck, Edward, (1963) *Changing Japan*, Holt, Rinehart and Winston, New York.

Index

Abbi, Behari L., 25
Abject product, 82
Adoption, 24
Adult marriage, 126
Age differences, 82
Age of marriage, 80-81
Agrawala community, 19
Ahir, 21
Allied phenomena, 20
Ancient philosophical postulation, 13
Anderson, Nel, 75
Anuloma marriage, 85, 99
Arrange marriages, 88-89, 109
Attitudinal dimensions, 26, 83, 86, 89, 102, 106, 115, 121, 122, 124, 129
Authority, centralised pattern of, 61-62

Bachmann, Hedvig, 58
Bangalore, 15
Baniyas, 21, 23
Basic organ, 14
Beteille, A., 112
Bhavnagar, 17
Bhumihars, 33
Biological factors, 38
Brahmins, 33
Bridegroom, participation of, 110; sellection of, 67-68
Burgess, E.W., 31

Caste categories, 21; cross-tabulation of, 15, 33
Caste systems, 112, 113
Cell, 13
Ceremonies, 115
Chamars, 21, 33, 99
Changing uniforms, 46, 129
Child care and control, 39
Chhibar, Y.P., 70
Chhoti Patan Devi, 27
Chitness, Suma, 114
Choice of bridegroom, 62
Christensen, Harold T., 14, 15
Chulah, 18
Classification, scheme for, 30-32
Co-education, acceptance of, 113, 118, 128; attitude of, 111-12; phenomenon of, 117
Collateral joint family, 30
Conklin, George H., 19
Cosmopolitanism, 75
Cox, O.C., 101
Cross-cultural regularities, 38
Customs, 101

Dahl, Robert A., 62
Dasgupta, Manisha, 129
Data collection, techniques of, 21-22; comparative of, 15
Daughter-in-law relationship, 54
Death rate, 26
Decision-making, individual pattern of, 66-67, 69
Democratization, 57
Desai, I.P., 17, 25, 48, 114
Deuteronomy ecclesiaster, 14
Deviation, 102
Dharmashala, 97
Dhobi, 21
Division of labour, 38, 40, 42, 49, 102; analysis of, 47; pattern of, 44
Divorce, legal provision of, 98
Dowry system, 81, 94, 114
Dube, S.C., 26, 39, 50, 51, 58

Dusadh, 21

Economic activity, 18, 39-41; factors, 75; status, 112, 129
Educated unemployment, problem of, 71-73
Education, 27, 65, 105; aspiration, 119-20; correlation of, 128; form of, 73; methods of, 114-16; new trends in, 16; types of, 74
Education and family types of, 34-35, 139
Educational accomplishments, 121-23; aspiration, 115; attainments, 34; categories, 119; opportunities, 115
Egalitarian, 68
Employment, 70, 105, 106
Endogamous marriage, 84, 126
Equalitarianism, 53, 60
Exploration, 35

Factors, 38, 96
Familial composition, 20; effectiveness, 61; obligations, observance of, 14, 19
Families, behaviour pattern in, 20; classification of, 33; economic status, 110
Family, definitions, 23-24; devision of labour, 131; interpersonal relationships, 132; power and authority in, 61, 133; types, income of, 33-36
Family planning, 16
Father-child relationship, 54, 64
Formal education, 116
Functions, constilation of, 25

Ganga, 27
Gangopadhayay, Bela, 80
Geographical isolation, 57
Ghurye, G.S., 102
Goode, W.J., 13, 14, 29, 38, 50, 61, 79, 81
Gore, M.S., 19, 38, 48, 50, 51, 56, 61, 114, 130
Grihastha-Ashrama, 79
Gurdwara, 27

Handling of money, 101-102
Harijan, 65
Harris, C.C., 24
Higher education, 119
Hindu marriage, traditional pattern of, 79; trends of, 84
Hindu social system, 14
Household duties, 39, 46
Husband-wife interaction pattern, 104-105; relationship of, 49-50
Hypergamous marriage, 85
Hypotheses, 20-21, 128

Individualization, 45
Industrialization, 15, 31, 39, 102, 103
Interaction, delineate pattern of, 48-49, 53; propinquity, 57-58
Inter-caste marriage, 9, 84-86; peculiarities, of, 88; practice of, 85; prevalence of, 126
Inter-personal relationship, 48-50
Intra-familial clashes, 16; interaction, 29
Issues, 62, 67

Japan, 49
Joint family, dissolution of, 31; economic activities, 42-43; obligation, 114; traditional form, 15, 17
Joint family system, 44; maintenance of, 36, 89; weakening of, 70

Kapadia, K.M., 26
Kaplan, Abraham, 62
Karve, Irawati, 14, 56, 79
Kashmiri Pandits, 17
Kayastha, 33
Khandan, 96
Kinship composition, 17; structure, 70; system, 114; terminology, 29
Kolenda, Pauline M., 30

Komarovsky, Mirra, 14, 22
Kotamb, 18
Kurmis, 21, 33, 88

Labour utilization, 19
Lambart, Richard D., 25
Language pattern, 115
Laswell, Harold D., 62
Libraries, 52
Limitations, 63
Lineal joint family, 31
Locke, H.J., 31
Love marriage, 88-89; performance of, 109
Lynch, Owen M., 25

MacIver, R.N., 13
Madan, T.N., 18
Madhya Pradesh, 87
Mahuva, 17
Mandelbaum, David G., 35
Marriage, change pattern of, 79-90, 136
Matching horoscopes, 93-94, 126; practice of, 108-110
Mathur, K.S., 84
Mead, Marget, 13
Mean age, 83-84
Middle range castes, 21
Mills, C. Wright, 62
Mode of living, 115
Modern education, 17
Modernization, 74, 99, 113
Morrisson, William A., 34
Mutual aid pattern, 59-60
Mutual obligation, 15, 17

Nimkoff, M.F., 31
Nuclear family, categories of, 30-32; desirability of, 16-17; preponderance of, 32
Nuclearization, 45
Numirical composition, 30

Objectives, 19-90, 62
Obligation, 15
Occupation, changing prestige of, 75-76
Occupational monopoly, 84; pattern, 70
Optimum employment, 118

Padri Ki Haveli, 27
Pandit, D.F., 70
Paranjpe, A.C., 101, 102
Parsons, Talcott, 31
Participation, 127; categories of, 91-92
Partition, 26
Pasi, 21
Pataliputra, 27
Patna, 26, 124
Patrilineal society, 26
Performance, pattern of, 40-41
Politico-jural functions, 18
Power-wielding pattern, 20, 61, 62, 67
Prabhu, P.N., 24, 79, 98, 114
Pratiloma marriage, 85, 99
Pre-pubertal marriage, 81, 115
Property, ownership of, 17
Proverbs, 14
Psalms, 14
Public meeting, 52
Purity and pollution, 101

Questionnare, 16, 22, 23

Rajputs, 33, 90
Ritual interaction, pattern, 115
Role collection, pattern of, 124
Ross, Aileen D., 15, 24, 30, 31, 56, 79, 114
Rural-urban variation, 16

Sachchidananda, 16, 115
Schooling of children, 62
Secular environment, 99
Secularization, 129
Segregation, 46; pattern of, 80
Sellection of bride, 105-106
Selltiz, Claire, 23
Semi structural schedule, 23
Sex-patterning, 39; segregation, 41
Sibling relationship, 124; institution, 13;

personalies, 48
Socialization pattern, 29
Socio-psychological environment, 127
Speculation, 14
Spouses, criteria in selection of, 93-96
Straus, A. Murray, 61
Structural functional approach, 19
Supplemented sub-nuclear, 30
Symbolic authority, 66

Task differentiation, pattern of, 20
Task performance, pattern of, 41-42
Traditional Hindu family, 68
Traditional Joint family, 29; maintenance of, 83
Traditional marriage pattern, 16, 96
Transformation, 31

Unemployment, 71, 72; acuteness problem of, 73, 78
Upper castes, characteristics of, 37
Urban Joint families, 18-19; composition of, 29-36; types of, 30
Urban setting, 15
Urbanization, 15, 31, 102, 113; growth of, 125; impact of, 18, 19
Uttarsu Umangiri, 18

Validity, 21

Waller, W., 14, 22
Weber, Max, 31
Widow marriage, prohibition of, 79
Women as money-earness, 76-77; occupational careers of, 78; responsibilities of, 39
Work and family, 135

Yadavas, 21, 33

Zamindari, 86